THE LUCKY CAPTAIN

THE LUCKY CAPTAIN

The Story of George W. Dow,
His Ancestors,
and 40 Years at Sea

William Dow Turner

SNOWMASS VILLAGE, COLORADO

The Lucky Captain
By William Dow Turner

Copyright © 2016 by William D. Turner

ISBN 978-0-9964454-3-6

DESIGN & MAPS © 2016 | CURT CARPENTER

PRINTED IN THE UNITED STATES

DOW TURNER
Box 6065 · Snowmass Village, Colorado 81615

CONTENTS

Author's Note ix

Acknowledgements xi

PART ONE | *Early Dows in the New World*

Transplanting to America 1

Watertown 5

Hampton 7

Salisbury 9

Deer Isle 14

Tremont/Mount Desert 19

Hancock 22

PART TWO | *George—Growing Up and Going to Sea*

George's Early Days 28

Becoming a Sailor 31

A Wife 33

Family in Ellsworth 36

A Career as a Captain 38

The *Stampede* 40

PART THREE | *Family and Seafaring in Melrose*

The *GEM* 47

Settling in Melrose 49

The *Albert L. Butler* 50

The *Auburndale* 52

Melrose Home Life 57

PART FOUR | *The* Lawson *and its Atlantic Crossing*

The Ship   65
Sailing to England   82
Scilly   88
Landfall   96
Morning   105
The Aftermath   116
Reflections   130

PART FIVE | *Toward Retirement*

Recuperation   140
A Little More Sailing   142
Melrose Retirement   145
Girard's Bizarre Saga   148
Passing of the Captain's Family   151

Epilogue

A Change of Course   155
The Captain as Captain   156
The Captain as a Man   157

Bibliography   161
Illustration Sources   170

For all the descendants of

GEORGE W. DOW

... already five generations and counting.

We live in his wake.

I N AUGUST OF 1999, Andrew, Nick, Paula, and I visited the Isles of Scilly, officially in the county of Cornwall, but 29 miles out to sea, west of Land's End, England.

The sailing ship *Thomas W. Lawson* ran aground and sank in those remote islands the night of Friday, December 13, 1907. The *Lawson* was the only seven-masted ship ever built, and it's fate "has become almost legend amongst seafarers and certainly amongst the island-ers of Scilly." The captain was George W. Dow, great grandfather and great-great grandfather of the three boys who visited Scilly in 1999.

That visit fuelled an interest in learning more about the captain. Thomas Hall's book, *The T.W. Lawson: The Fate of the World's Only Seven-Masted Schooner*, published in 2003, and David Quinn's historical narrative *Leviathan's Master: The Wreck of the World's Largest Sailing Ship*, published in 2009, shed more light on the cap-tain and especially his fateful voyage aboard the *Lawson*. And, in the fall of 2015, John Hicks's volume, *An Absolute Wreck: the loss of the Thomas W. Lawson*, brought more detail and analysis of the Atlantic crossing and the events and people affected by the ship-wreck. All three of these books are well researched and cover Dow and the *Lawson* on its final voyage very well. The other 71 years of Captain Dow's life, however, remained little known and undocu-mented, even within the Dow family.

This volume describes more of the captain's ancestry and life story, as we know it, ranging back to the first Dows to migrate to America nearly 400 years ago, and continuing to the captain's grandchildren in the late 20th century. This is not a novel, and no events, action, or dialogue have been invented. It is also a work in process, with family members

Andrew (l), Nick(r), and I at the Isles of Scilly, 1999

still trying to discover more and fill the remaining gaps.

There are great spans of time, especially prior to the formation of American states, with almost no written history and no solid records of the Dows in Massachusetts and what is now New Hampshire and Maine. Even birth certificates were not common until about 1875. Seven generations of Dows lived in America before George Washington was sworn in as the first President of the United States.

With so little to go on, the task has proved rewarding but remarkably difficult and time-consuming. As a result, I have limited my focus to a single line—the captain's direct male ancestors and descendants, and their immediate families. This admittedly has produced a narrow, incomplete, and sexist picture.

There remain more fascinating discoveries to be made by others who care to embark on broadening the genealogical story of the family, both to the 14 wives and 80 children cited in this story and their families, and also to the five generations descending from the captain that are already in place. ⚓

—WDT | AUGUST 5, 2016

ACKNOWLEDGEMENTS

S ITTING IN MY OFFICE in Hong Kong in August 2004, I received an email from Richard (Dick) Calderone— whom I did not know and who turned out to be my third cousin— inquiring if I were related to a Captain George Dow, who was his great grand uncle. My reply that the captain was indeed my great grandfather, led to Dick and his wife Nancy providing me with a trove of genealogical data, especially regarding lineage all the way back to 16th century Dows in England. The results of their hard work and documentation provided a backbone for my research and are very much appreciated. We miss Dick, who passed away in the summer of 2015.

Dick recommended that I also contact David Quinn, a retired businessman living in Prescott, Arizona, who writes historical fiction and was researching the Captain and the *Lawson*. I did so and discovered that David is also my third cousin, one of the Captain's other brothers being his great grandfather. David and his wife Betsy became our good friends, and I am indebted to them for the swapping of research results and perspectives over these years, as well as for David's excellent book, already acknowledged.

Thomas Hall, who lives in Scituate, Massachusetts, on part of the former estate of the financier Thomas W. Lawson, for whom the giant schooner was named, helped and encouraged me early on in my research. His comprehensive book about the *Lawson* and its demise is a primer for anyone wanting a thorough and extensively illustrated history. Shortly after its publication, we participated together in a meeting at the Hancock Historical Society, in the Captain's early hometown of Hancock, Maine. Tom's many dives onto the *Lawson* and knowledge of every detail provide a unique perspective for which I am grateful.

Lois Crabtree Johnson, the long-time and now-retired curator of the Historical Society of the Town of Hancock provided many unique and often first-hand insights into the Captain's family history in both the Town of Hancock and Hancock County. My several visits with her at the Town Hall and at her home, along with phone conversations and written correspondence, were invaluable in helping me to piece together and understand the lives of the captain's family, including his parents, uncles, wife, children, business partners, homes, and other aspects of their times in Hancock and Ellsworth in the mid-1800's. Her wit and delight in discovering and conveying something new has been a high point of my work.

Finally, the many museums and libraries all over Maine and in Boston; Mystic, Connecticut; Annapolis, Maryland; Newport News, Virginia; St. Mary's, Isles of Scilly; and elsewhere— most of them cited in the Bibliography—were invaluable, both as stores of facts and history, and also with staffs who were dedicated to helping me. ⚓

"*Captain Dow was one of the best ship masters that the State of Maine had produced.*"

—T. C. MOON
STAMPEDE'S FIRST MATE | 1875

PART 1

Early Dows in the New World

Less than two decades after the Mayflower *and its load of
a hundred immigrant passengers landed at Plymouth Rock,
29-year-old Henry Dow leaves his village of Ormsby
in northeast England and heads for a new life
in the New World.*

TRANSPLANTING TO AMERICA

THE PURITAN MOVEMENT to 'purify' and reform the
Church of England and its lockstep relationship with
the British Crown led to the Pilgrim journey on the *Mayflower*
in 1620 and the settlement at Plymouth, Massachusetts. The
conflict gained momentum when King Charles I dissolved the
British Parliament in 1629, further raising the religious and
political hostility. As a result, the decade of the 1630's saw
80,000 people leave England, with 20,000 of them coming to
New England and establishing the Massachusetts Bay Colony
at what is now metropolitan Boston. This Great Migration
continued until 1640, when Charles II reconvened Parliament,
British attention turned more toward Europe, and the rate of
exodus from England fell sharply.

Those leaving Britain for America were a group with an uncharacteristic profile. Most were middle class families, with some education and from all parts of England, but with more than half coming from the eastern counties of Norfolk, Suffolk, and Essex. They were motivated by religious concerns and a desire to live more pious and worthy lives in America, rather than to improve their economic status. In fact, these families in general were relatively skilled, with more than half artisans or craftsman in England, and as a result were relatively prosperous and stable. The literacy rate was perhaps twice that of England as a whole. Few were rich (the rich being reluctant to pick up and desert their sources of wealth and comfort), and few were poor (the poor lacking economic confidence and unable to afford the trip to America). The typical family profile was a married couple in their 30's, accompanied by three or more children with potential for more, and with few if any servants. Approximately 17% came as servants, compared to the 75% of Virginia's population that arrived as servants.

The impact of the English immigrants and settlements on New England and, indeed, on America, was magnified by the fact that in the three years immediately preceding the 1620 Plymouth landing, smallpox had killed 90% of the Native Americans in Massachusetts Bay territory.

The demographics of this wave of immigrants brought to the Massachusetts Colony a somewhat homogeneous, multi-generational, hard-working, and family-centric population, bound further together as a group by the daunting eight-to-ten-week voyage from their home ports to the Boston area.

HENRY (B. 1605)

H ENRY DOW and his family matched this profile. He was born in Runham parish, England, in October of 1605 (some records say 1608), and in 1637 was living with Joan, his wife of six years, four children, and a 17-year-old girl servant, Ann Manning, in nearby Ormsby (sometimes Ormesby), in the county of Norfolkshire.

The surname Dow is of ancient English origin, dating back to the very beginning of the use of family names. And, Henry was at least the fourth generation of Dows residing in that area of Norfolkshire. His great grandfather John Dow was born about 1500 in the small village of Tylner, west of Runham. He married Johan Coop, was "thrifty and had a house," and had three children. John's eldest son Thomas was born in 1528, also in Tylner, but moved to and lived most of his life in

Mayflower II is a replica of the 17th-century ship *Mayflower*, celebrated for transporting the Pilgrims to the New World in 1620.

Runham, marrying Margaret England of Runham and having seven children. And, Thomas's first son Henry, born in 1550, spent his life there, marrying Elizabeth March and having eight children, including our subject Henry, who was with wife Joan and family at Ormsby in 1637.

At least the last three of these generations in England were somewhat well to do, possessing land, some education, and religion. The first Henry was the parish clerk and then warden and had inherited at least 14 acres of land from his mother. And, at least from Thomas onwards, the families owned several parcels of land in the area, some of which may have been granted by the King in recognition of military service.

During the 16th century and into the 17th, these four English generations were said to progress from Catholicism through the Reformation into the Church of England. The last Henry— our Henry—was "probably the [family's] only dissenter, surely the only Puritan."

And, it seems that the plague epidemic of 1579, which swept Europe and took the lives of more than one third of the Norfolk population, had missed the Dows, probably owing to their rural locations.

In the spring of 1637, Henry applied for permission for the family to emigrate to America. (Joan had been widowed from her first husband, Roger Nudd, of Ormsby, and she brought a five year old and an infant to the Henry Dow family.) They were members of the Church of England but had become greatly dissatisfied with the dogma and corruption in the Church and

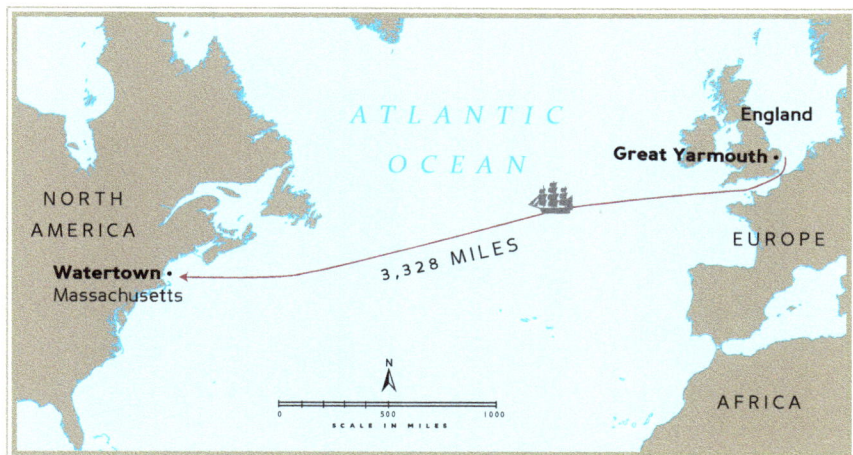

Henry Dow family sails from Great Yarmouth, England to Boston/Watertown, Massachusetts in 1637.

its links with the British Crown. They were granted a license on April 11, 1637, "to pass into New England, to inhabit." Henry was 32 years old and Joan 30, and they would eventually have 10 children.

They made the trip late that spring, traveling the 7½ miles from their home in Ormsby to board a ship to Massachusetts at the Great Yarmouth docks, one of the ports of departure along the English coast. Six other families from the parish accompanied the Dows to try the New World. Henry and family would be the first of the name Dow in America.

WATERTOWN

ARRIVING IN BOSTON harbor, they made their way to settle in Watertown, just west of Boston and at the time the second most populous town in the growing territory of

1627 English Village, Plymouth, Massachusetts

Massachusetts. Watertown had been founded in 1630 by Sir Richard Saltonstall, a Yorkshireman who led a group of English settlers up the Charles River to settle there. Watertown at the time was quite large, encompassing land that today lies within the towns of Cambridge, Weston, Waltham, Lincoln, and Belmont. Watertown had the first gristmill in the colony, and over the next few decades, became the main horse and cattle market in New England, and also was home to one of the first woolen mills in America.

Within a year of arriving in the Massachusetts Colony and settling in Watertown, Henry was admitted as a Freeman on May 2, 1638, signifying his acceptance and commitment that he and his family had found their new home. Less than a year later, on March 20, 1639, Henry and Joan had the first Dow child born in America, son Joseph.

The next year, in June of 1640, Joan Dow died, and the following year, Henry married widow Margaret Cole of Dedham,

Massachusetts. They added three sons and two daughters to the family over the next 16 years.

HAMPTON

F OLLOWING HIS MARRIAGE to Margaret, Henry acquired several tracts of land for a farm, along with a house, in the town of Hampton. The purchase (from a John Saunders) of previously-cleared land for farming was an advantage for Henry in putting together a new homestead in Hampton, and the family moved there in early 1644. In his seven years in Watertown, Henry had become a moderate capitalist. This homestead remained with Henry's descendants for more than two centuries, until 1854 when it was sold and passed into other hands.

The town of Hampton, 60 miles north of Watertown, was settled only in 1638 and incorporated the next year—one of 23 new towns founded in Massachusetts during the 1630's. The area was referred to as the Upper Plantation and encompassed Seabrook, Danville, Sandown, and other surrounding villages. Although Hampton was later to become part of Rockingham County, New Hampshire, in 1639 the area was under the authority of Massachusetts Bay Colony.

Hampton was part of the early settlement expansion to the north from Boston. And the family's move to Hampton and the Atlantic coast was the first of eight generations of Dows moving northward to central Maine over the next 200 years.

During the 1640's and 1650's, Henry served in several elected and appointed positions of leadership, including as a Hampton selectman, a deputy from Hampton to the General Court of Massachusetts, and with an appointment to examine and record all land grants and highways. He died in Hampton on April 21, 1659, at age 53, some years before wife Margaret, who married again in 1661 and moved to Ipswich.

JOSEPH (B. 1639)

ENRY'S SON JOSEPH, born in Watertown on March 20, 1639, was the first Dow born in America, moved with his family to Hampton at age five, and spent the rest of his life there. Like his father, Joseph was active in town affairs, and was appointed to represent the town before the "royal council" on land claim disputes resulting from conflicting land-grant charters.

Joseph became a Quaker at age 34, and moved to the southern part of Hampton, now known as Seabrook. He was among the early converts in this country to the Quaker sect founded and led in England by George Fox. Perhaps his conversion was prompted—or at least reinforced—by Fox's visit to the American colonies between 1671 and 1673. With his conversion, Joseph largely withdrew from his earlier high-profile public life.

Although he and others associated with this Quaker mission suffered some degrees of public persecution, Joseph's outspokenness and persistence in demanding their rights led to a dampening of the criticism and better acceptance and treatment of the area's Quaker population. In 1701, he was one of the trustees to whom town land was conveyed (and to some extent purchased by him) for "all those Christian people, called Quakers, living in Hampton, to seat a meeting house thereon." Joseph died two years later, in 1703, at age 64. His wife, Mary Sanborn, lived another 29 years, dying in 1732 at age 87. Joseph and Mary had married when he was 23 and she was 17, and she also remained a consistent Quaker.

Joseph was widely known for importing and putting to use some fine items from England, including the first steel animal trap in America, and the best compass available. He was the first of four generations in his line of Dows to adopt the Quaker life.

JOSEPH (B. 1663)

JOSEPH AND MARY named their first son Joseph. He was born on October 20, 1663, and they had 8 more sons and 3 daughters over the next 25 years.

SALISBURY

THE YOUNGER JOSEPH became a sergeant in the anti-Indian militia and saw considerable Indian fighting. He was also a weaver. He lived his life in the same area, perhaps moving among Hampton, Seabrook, and Salisbury—a span of about 20 miles along the coast between the Merrimack and Piscataqua rivers. He married Mary Challis (5 years his junior) in May 1687, with the wedding taking place in the adjoining town of Amesbury. She joined the Quakers, or "friends," and they had four sons and a daughter. Mary and the last child, a daughter also named Mary—died on the same day only three days after the baby's birth in 1697.

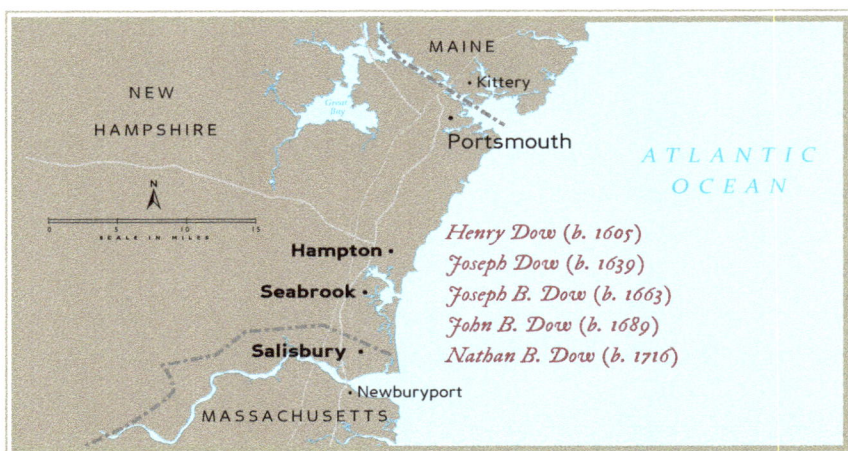

MAINE
• Kittery

NEW
HAMPSHIRE

Portsmouth

ATLANTIC
OCEAN

Hampton •

Seabrook •

Salisbury •

Henry Dow (b. 1605)
Joseph Dow (b. 1639)
Joseph B. Dow (b. 1663)
John B. Dow (b. 1689)
Nathan B. Dow (b. 1716)

• Newburyport
MASSACHUSETTS

After seven years in Watertown, the Henry Dow's move
60 miles north to Hampton, New Hampshire, an area
where the next four Dow generations would reside.

Joseph married again about a year later in Seabrook, and he
and second wife Hannah had four more children between
1705 and 1719. There was a distinct shift toward the biblical
in naming the two sets of children. Mary's were Joseph, John,
James, Philip, and Mary, whereas Hannah's were Eliphaz,
Noah, Bildad, and Judah. No doubt this reflects a shift in
religious beliefs and importance in family affairs. Paradoxically,
however, the children of the first wife, all more or less austere
Quakers, were horrified by what seemed to them the wild
life of the family of second wife Hannah Dow—despite the
biblical names.

A child of Indian parents, Hannah had been raised by a
Seabrook Quaker family as a Christian, with full knowledge and permission of her birth parents. This was the only
recorded "mixed marriage" in Seabrook. Joseph remained a

Quaker after his second marriage, but laxly. And, no love was lost when Mary's son John showed up to administer the estate of their father Joseph when he died in 1734 at age 70.

Joseph's Seabrook farm home was near those of his brothers Jeremiah and Henry, the three being owners of a single property originally owned by their father.

Joseph was the first to spot the Indians in the great raid of August 17, 1703, and he ran to give the alarm to the nearest blockhouse. This raid was engineered by the French government of Canada, and, interestingly, no harm came to Joseph's family, perhaps due to Joseph's Indian wife.

JOHN (B. 1689)

JOSEPH AND MARY'S second son, John, was born on December 16, 1689, in Hampton. He lived in Salisbury and South Hampton all his life and had 10 children, distributed among three wives. In early 1714, at age 24, he married Dinah Severance, and they had three children. John, Dinah, and their children were "more or less austere Quakers."

Dinah died not long after bearing her third child in 1718, and John married Mary Challis—a second cousin—the next year. John and Mary had five daughters and a son over 16 years. Records show John buying a Salisbury farm in 1731, although by then he had lived away from his father's Hampton house for some years. Upon Mary's death in 1737 or 1738, John married his third wife, widow Elizabeth Simonds, in early 1739, and they had a daughter the next year. Elizabeth had been married to John Simonds of Haverhill for more than 30 years and had a grown family there. John Dow died in South Hampton sometime after 1758, at least 69 years old.

There is one opinion that John's children all were by Dinah and that the marriages to Mary Challis and Elizabeth Simonds did not occur. However, the record appears to show that Dinah died in 1718, and that seven of John's children were born over the subsequent 22 years.

NATHAN (B. 1716)

NATHAN DOW, John and Dinah's first son, was born August 6, 1716 in Salisbury. Nathan, a Quaker, married Mary (also called Sarah) Flanders in 1739, at age 23, and they lived around Salisbury or Haverhill for the next 20 years, having seven children.

Beginning with his marriage to Mary, who refused to join the Society of Friends and become a Quaker, Nathan's family had a serious falling out with the church. (This may have caused a three-year delay in baptizing their first child Jeremiah.) As a result, Nathan left the Salisbury/Haverhill area in 1760 and moved his wife and seven children up the coast toward Maine. It is unclear whether anyone in lower Massachusetts heard from them again.

During the first half of the 18th century, the religiously intolerant Puritans of Massachusetts considered the lands to the East of Essex County, and certainly beyond the Hampton and Piscataqua rivers, to be the "Devil's own", populated by "godless Indians and papist French." But, from about 1765, the fear

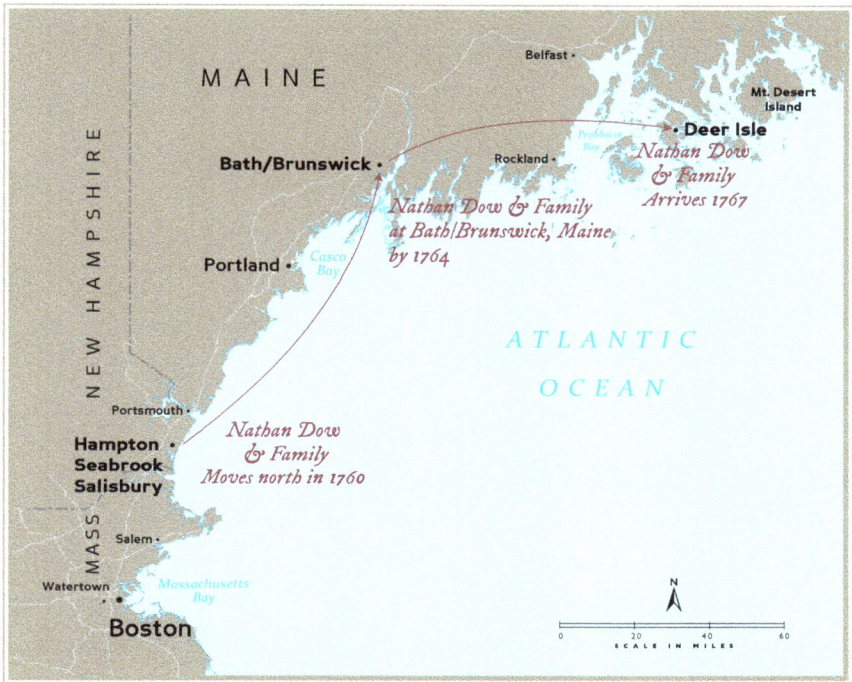

After four generations along the New Hampshire shore, Nathan Dow moves his family up the Maine Coast, arriving at Deer Isle in 1767.

and hysteria of eastern expansion gave way to a perception of opportunity and freedom, and English families began a serious migration eastward. Nathan Dow's family was an early participant in that migration.

The falling out with the Massachusetts Quakers not only drove the Nathan Dows from Massachusetts and up to Maine, but also appears to have driven the family away from the Society of Friends. The importance of religion in their daily lives, and certainly the role of Quaker faith and behavior, appear to have diminished or vanished from Nathan's family and subsequent generations of Dows.

DEER ISLE

ALTHOUGH THE FAMILY SETTLED on Deer Isle, Maine, they took about seven years to get there. In 1762, Major William Eaton, led a group from Haverill, Massachusetts, to be the original settlers on Deer Isle. Rather than having religious issues with the church, their case for leaving centered on a desire for more farmland to support their families than was available around Haverill. To some, it had become "emigrate or starve."

Maine was virtually uninhabited. And, the end of the French and Indian war in 1762 meant that it was newly safe to go there. Deer Isle seemed the Promised Land, simply in terms of a safe place with plenty of food. The island was named for its abundance of deer, fish was plentiful, timber abundant, and the land would be fertile when cleared. Land was theirs just by occupying it, and the rock coast discouraged potential enemies from landing. (There was no bridge from Deer Isle to the mainland until 1939!)

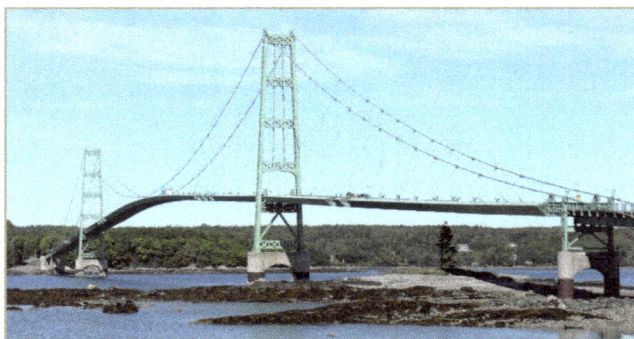

The first bridge connecting Deer Isle with the mainland was opened in 1939.

So, here in the mid-1760's, on a 124-square-mile island, some 175 miles up the Atlantic coast from Salisbury, settled about 30 families from Haverill, Gloucester, and a few from the Salisbury area.

The Dows had left Salisbury two years before, in 1760, and were not part of Eaton's group. Rather, they moved up the Maine coast gradually until 1767, when they finally reached Deer Isle. Virtually all northward travel—including Eaton's—was by water, since there was no overland route. Little is known about how, where, and when the Dow family made their way, except that in 1764, Nathan was living not far from Bath and Brunswick, probably up the New Meadows or Kennebec River on the mainland.

One of the channels of the New Meadows River
up from Casco Bay

Three years later, in the fall of 1767, they arrived on Deer Isle, making Nathan the first Dow of Deer Isle, referred to as "the Quaker born from old Salisbury." He settled on a significant piece of land bordering on Northwest Harbor, and containing what came to be known as Dow Point, on the northwest side of the entrance to the harbor. Nathan may have died soon after reaching Deer Isle, because his will was being probated on May 13, 1767.

Nathan Dow was among the first Deer Isle settlers with farmland between present-day Dow Road and Dow Point.

At Nathan's death, his sons Nathan and John were 21 and 13, respectively. Young Nathan was executor of his father's estate and lived a long life on the inherited farm today still known as Dow Point. And, there is evidence that Nathan also received a grant of land in the early 1780's, following a stint in the army in 1777. His neighbor was Jonathan Eaton, who came from the mainland with the elder Nathan Dow in 1767 (probably from the Brunswick/Bath area), and who married one of young Nathan's sisters, Diane (or Diana).

JOHN (B. 1754)

NATHAN SR. AND MARY'S LAST CHILD, John, was baptized in early November 1754, and by the time the family reached Deer Isle in 1767, John had spent more than half his young life en route from Salisbury.

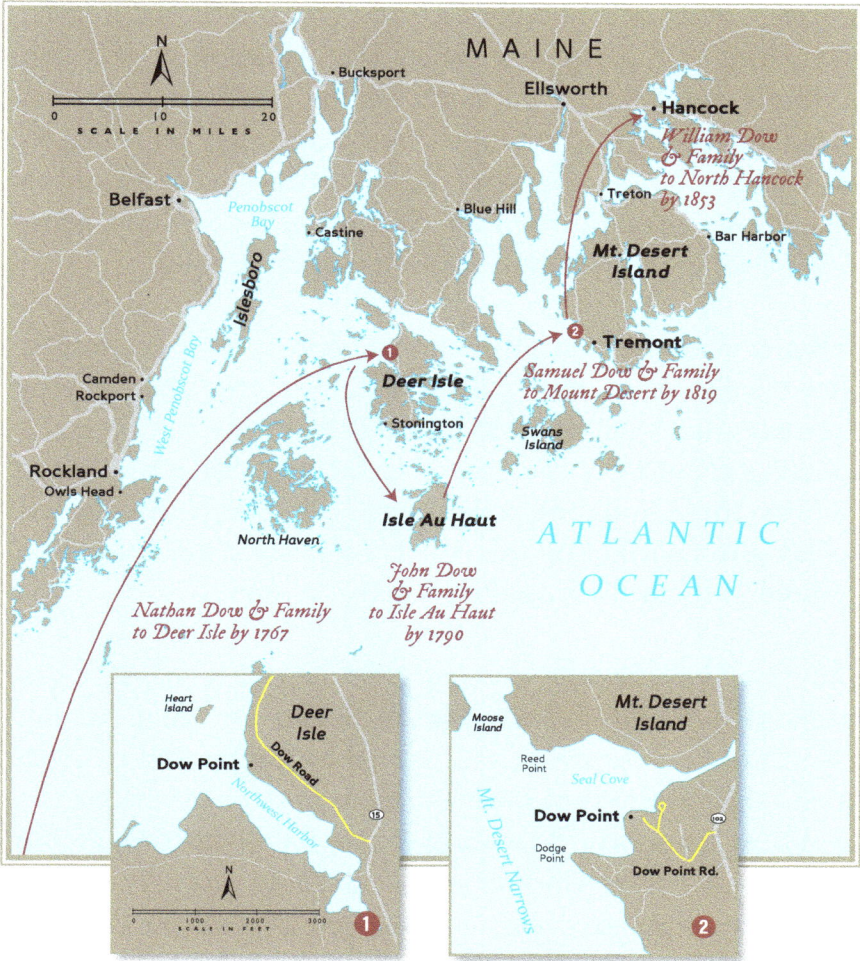

MAINE

- Bucksport
- Ellsworth
- Hancock
  - *William Dow & Family to North Hancock by 1853*
- Treton
- Belfast
- *Penobscot Bay*
- Blue Hill
- Castine
- Bar Harbor
- **Mt. Desert Island**
- *Islesboro*
- Camden
- Rockport
- ① **Deer Isle**
- ② • **Tremont**
  - *Samuel Dow & Family to Mount Desert by 1819*
- Stonington
- Swans Island
- Rockland
- Owls Head
- *West Penobscot Bay*
- North Haven
- **Isle Au Haut**
  - *John Dow & Family to Isle Au Haut by 1790*
- *Nathan Dow & Family to Deer Isle by 1767*

ATLANTIC OCEAN

SCALE IN MILES: 0 10 20

Inset ①:
- Heart Island
- **Deer Isle**
- Dow Point
- *Dow Road*
- *Northwest Harbor*
- 15
- N
- SCALE IN FEET: 0 1000 2000 3000
- ①

Inset ②:
- Moose Island
- **Mt. Desert Island**
- Reed Point
- *Seal Cove*
- **Dow Point**
- Dodge Point
- *Mt. Desert Narrows*
- Dow Point Rd.
- 102
- ②

From Deer Isle, three generations of Dow's move from the islands inland to Hancock by 1853.

He married Betty Saunders, from a Deer Isle family, in about 1778, and they had four sons and then five daughters over the ensuing 21 years. John was listed as a corporal in the Massachusetts contingent in the Revolutionary War.

Although Nathan had split with the Quakers in moving far away, and son John had joined the American revolutionary army, this was not the norm among the Dows of greater Massachusetts. For although Dows accounted for some 55 enlistments in Massachusetts regiments during the American Revolution, virtually none of this branch of Dows—many being Quakers at the time—assumed fighting roles.

There is evidence that John and the family, by 1790, settled on a nearby island, then called Shamm Island, a six mile by two mile island just six miles south across the water from the southern tip of Deer Isle. John recruited six other families to join him there, and the small group of colonists petitioned the Legislature continually that the ownerless island should be granted to them. This finally occurred in 1802.

The island's name was changed then to Holt's Island, a bastardization of the French Isle au Haute, or "high island," which had been explored and named by Captain John Smith in 1614. Isle au Haute has the highest point of land among the islands of Penobscot Bay—namely Mount Champlain at 540 feet above sea level. Until 1874, Isle au Haute was part of Deer Island Plantation, so it would be expected for all the Dows to be on record as being born and living at Deer Isle.

It is not known if the John Dow family returned to Deer Isle later in life, only that John and Betty Dow both passed away in November of 1835, perhaps from the same accident or sickness. John was 81.

Isle au Haute, just six miles in the distance from the tip of Deer Isle

SAMUEL (B. 1787)

JOHN AND BETTY'S fourth son, Samuel, was born on Deer Isle on May 11, 1787. He married Mary Stewart of Deer Isle about 1815, and they had six daughters and six or seven sons. Besides being a farmer, Samuel was a sailor and sea captain, the first of many in his family line.

TREMONT/MOUNT DESERT

BY 1819, Samuel, Mary, and their first two sons (Charles H. and Samuel T.) had moved from Deer Isle to a larger island, 15 miles to the northeast and close to the mainland, called Mount Desert. They settled at a spot on the southwest shore called Tremont, which still is marked by Dow Point and Dow Point Road along that coastline. Mary died in 1855 just before her 61st birthday, and Samuel six years later at age 74. Both are buried in Seal Cove Cemetery in Tremont.

WILLIAM (B. 1820)

The Tremont area settled by the Dows before 1820 still is marked by Dow Point Road leading to Dow Point Farm.

MAINE'S NAME was formalized by King Charles I in 1639, as a compliment to his wife and queen Henrietta Maria, who owned the province of Maine in France. On March 15, 1820, the District of Maine became a state, as part of a compromise by the U.S. Congress to maintain a balance between pro-slavery and anti-slavery states, whereby Missouri was also granted statehood, but as pro-slave. Eight months before, Massachusetts had agreed to Maine's becoming an independent state as a result of a vote by Maine inhabitants, in which 3,315 voted for separation, and 1,394 against. (The votes in Hancock County—1,581 for and 820 against—totaled half of all Maine votes, although some counties did not send in returns.)

Samuel and Mary's fourth son, William Hamilton Dow, was born in Tremont, in the new State of Maine, on June 1, 1820. William was a sea captain and also a gardener-farmer in Tremont. On September 8, 1839, he married Naomi Somes

Ober, when neither of them was yet 20 years old. Naomi was part of the Somes and Ober families that originally settled Mt. Desert Island. Somes Sound, Somesville, Ober Mill Road, and other places on the island are named for their families. William worked for Naiomi's father as a gardener-farmer in Pretty Marsh, near Bartlett's Landing in

Mount Desert. But, he also had become a seaman by the time he married, and three of his brothers and two of his uncles also were career mariners. All were farmers as well.

Naomi ran the Balm of Gideon Inn nearby on the County Road in North Hancock, and her father may have owned it. In the summers, boys from Boston University stayed at the Inn.

About 1832, a third cousin of William Dow, Alexander Dow, moved from Deer Isle to Searsport, Maine, as a farmer. His sons, Jonathan and Leroy began another noted seafaring branch of the Maine Dows. Captain Jonathan Dow, the most prominent one of his line, and his brother Leroy and son Amos all became sea captains, plying trade routes and ports around the world for several decades. After captaining many vessels, including the *Albatross, Atlantic,* and *Arletta*, Jonathan died on board the *Clarissa B. Carver* in San Francisco in 1879, and his brother took over as master for another five years, until the *Carver* was lost in a collision with a British steamer near Kobe, Japan. One vessel, the brig *Clytie,* saw all three of these

Somes Sound as seen from the small village of Somesville.

Dows as her successive captains, Jonathan from 1866 to 1870, then brother Leroy from 1870 to 1879, and finally son Amos from 1879 to 1882. Many other descendants of this branch of Dows were sea captains as well.

William and Naomi had four children while the family lived on a large farm in Tremont. They eventually had 10 children—six daughters and four sons—with seven of them living past age 68, and five into their 80's and 90's, uncommon longevity for the times.

In 1850, William's brother Samuel was 64 years old and still living on a large Tremont farm—at least 485 acres—with his wife Mary, and their four youngest children.

HANCOCK

BY 1850, however, oldest brother Charles had moved from Tremont on Mount Desert Island to the Town of Hancock, about 20 miles north and on the mainland. Charles Dow had a house with a Mansard roof on the north side of County Road (also called the Ellsworth Road, and now Route 1), overlooking the Taunton River near the ferry dock.

The Town of Hancock was incorporated in 1828 and had a population of 960 in 1850. Hancock County and the Town of Hancock were named for John Hancock, who had been President of the Continental Congress in 1775 to 1777, and was the most prominent governor of the Commonwealth of Massachusetts, within which Maine was contained until 1820. He applied his large signature to both the Declaration of

Independence and the Constitution, one of only six statesmen to have signed both documents.

During the early 1850's, brothers Samuel and William followed Charles to live in Hancock. William Dow's house was on County Road in North Hancock, across the street from Samuel's house. As land was cleared on the mainland, and new roads allowed more convenient travel on foot and horseback, homes and farms spread from central and south Hancock west along County Road toward Ellsworth. Instead of building homes solely along the shore to access coastal transportation, homes were now also built along inland roads, thus populating North Hancock and inland Maine.

The three Dow brothers (Charles, Samuel, and William) were among the families who came to central Maine during the early- and mid-19th century to join the earlier first settlors in developing the town's and county's enterprise, which comprised family farms, fishing, ship-building, and ice, lime, and granite harvesting. It was not until the late 1800's that Hancock began to grow through intermarriages with families "from away."

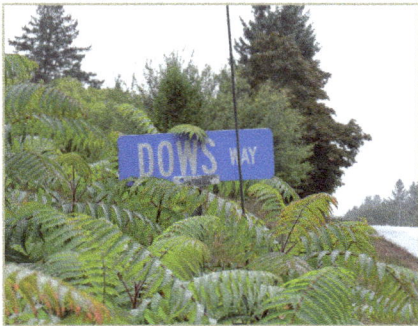

The long driveway adjoining Charles Dow's home on County Road in the 1850s is still named Dows Way.

The move off Mount Desert Island and inland to Hancock reflected the improving roads and bridges, the growth and industry of nearby Ellsworth, and, for the three Dow brothers, a move away from farming. It did not, however, lead to a diminished commitment to seafaring, as all three brothers were career mariners, captaining vessels as a primary occupation.

All settlors and visitors to Hancock arrived in some kind of vessel, because there were no other means of transportation and virtually no roads to and from the area. And from early on, water vessels of all kinds and sizes were built there. Between 1838 and 1876, at least 30 vessels were built in Hancock alone— five brigs and 25 schooners, ranging from 24 to 224 tons. As the local history book sums up:

> Hancock owes its early prosperity and its later success as a town to the ships, ship operators and the men who manned them. They all brought money and culture into the town.

In 1853, William Dow joined with local businessmen Asa Wasgatt and Leonard Higgins to rebuild the 1829, 81-ton schooner *Fulcrum* in Hancock. The vessel was 67 feet long, 20 feet wide and drew eight feet of water. Wasgatt owned half, and the other two a quarter each. William was the captain, and Hancock was the schooner's home port. Building or rebuilding a ship locally, with the captain taking a partial ownership interest, was the custom of the times along the New England coast, and continued into the early 20th century. William Dow served as the *Fulcrum*'s master from the launch in 1853 into the 1860's.

From the 1860's onward, Hancock men would fish the Grand Banks of Newfoundland from May to September, dry and pack their 100-ton codfish cargoes in Hancock, and then carry them—often on the same vessels—to the West Indies and Brazil. The industry of shipbuilding, fishing on the Grand Banks, drying and packing the fish in Hancock, and delivering cargoes to ports far away was a major source of employment in Hancock. (However, after one schooner was lost with its crew of many Hancock boys, it was ruled that not more than one third of a vessel's crew could hail from the same town.)

Beyond Grand Banks fishing and shipping fish to the Caribbean and ports farther south, Hancock vessels, captains, and crews sailed in the commercial trade to Europe as well. Many of the local sea captains owned shares in their vessels and shared in the profits, and taxes on the vessels provided the town with a healthy source of revenue.

By 1878, however, the Survey of Hancock County noted, "The future of this town, as of the county, is in its water power, its stone, and its ice."

From the 1840's onward, shipyards in southeastern Maine had built the bulk of the nation's fast, square-rigged clipper ships that made record-setting voyages carrying goods and passengers to and from Gold Rush-era California, Australia and the Far East. Between 1850 and 1856 alone, 89 were launched in Maine, mostly in yards from Bucksport south to Kittery. But, by the late 1850's, economic conditions favored ships with greater cargo capacity and smaller crews on the high seas, so clipper construction basically ceased.

Although schooner and other vessel construction continued during the last half of the 19th century, both the number and the tonnage of new vessels built in Maine peaked in the late 1850's. In the five-year period 1852-57, 2,003 vessels were built, weighing some 874,000 tons. But by 1885-90, production had fallen 80% to 415 vessels totaling 210,000 tons.

During the Civil War, between 1861 and 1864, Confederate "commerce raiders" made a dent in the supply of Maine vessels by capturing 88 of them, from off the coast of Maine and Nova Scotia, down the Atlantic coast and the Caribbean to Trinidad. Most were burned, sunk, or otherwise destroyed, with only seven eventually released to their rightful owners.

As with shipbuilding, Maine's trade overall had begun to fall off as well. One measure—shipping tonnage in Maine—plateaued at an average of about 800,000 tons per year during the 15 years from 1855 to 1870, and then declined rapidly by more than half to 374,000 tons in 1890. ⚓

A summary of ten generations preceding and following
Captain George W. Dow, from 1605–1961, is as follows:

DESCENDANTS		SELECTED CONTEMPORARY WORLD EVENTS
Henry Dow	Born 10/5/1605 Ormsby, England Died 4/21/1659 Hampton, NH 2 wives, 7 children	Galileo improves telescope, advances astronomy 1609 Michelangelo dies 1610 Thirty Year's War devastates Europe 1618-48 Shakespeare's first works 1623 Charles I King of England 1625-49; religious struggles Taj Mahal building starts 1632
Joseph Dow	Born 3/20/1639 Watertown, MA Died 4/4/1703 Hampton, NH 1 wife, 12 children	Louis XIV rules France 1643-1715 Great Plague and Great Fire in London 1665-66
Joseph Dow	Born 10/20/1663 Hampton, NH Died 2/5/1735 Salisbury, MA 2 wives, 9 children	Charles II King of England 1660-85 Rembrandt dies 1669 Newton presents his three laws of motion 1686
John Dow	Born 12/16/1689 Hampton, NH Died 1758 Salisbury, MA 3 wives, 10 children	William III King of England 1689-94 Salem witch trials in Massachusetts 1692
Nathan Dow	Born 8/6/1716 Salisbury, MA Died 5/13/1767 Deer Isle, ME 1 wife, 7 children	George I King of England 1714-27 French and Indian War 1754-63 Brown University founded 1764
John Dow	Born 11/10/1754 Salisbury, MA Died 11/1835 Deer Isle, ME 1 wife, 9 children	George III King of England 1760-1820 American Revolutionary War 1775-83 Declaration of Independence adopted 1776 U.S. Constitution ratified 1788 French Revolution 1789-99
Samuel Dow	Born 5/11/1787 Deer Isle, ME Died 10/31/1861 Mt Desert. ME 1 wife, 7 children	Presidents: Washington, Adams. Jefferson, Madison Catherine the Great Empress of Russia 1762-96 U.S. declares war for the first time 1812 Napoleon defeated at Battle of Waterloo 1815
William H. Dow	Born 6/1/1820 Mt. Desert. ME Died 9/25/1894 Gouldsboro, ME 1 wife, 10 children	Presidents: Monroe, Adams, Jackson, van Buren, Harrison, Tyler Maine and Massachusetts granted statehood 1820 Samuel Morse demonstrates the telegraph 1838 Irish potato famine 1845-51

George W. Dow	Born 11/1847 Mt Desert, ME
	Died 3/17/1919 Melrose, MA
	1 wife, 4 children
		Presidents: Polk, Taylor, Fillmore, Pierce, Buchanan,
		    Lincoln, Johnson. Grant, Hayes, Garfield. Arthur,
		    Cleveland, Harrison, McKinley, T. Roosevelt, Taft,
		    Wilson
		Gold discovered in California 1848
		Oil drilled in Titusville, Pennsylvania 1859
		U.S. Civil War 1861-65
		Bell patents the telephone 1876
		Edison invents incandescent light bulb 1879
		Ford Motor Company formed by Henry Ford 1903
		Wright Brothers make first flight at Kitty Hawk 1903
		World War I 1914-19

Richard E. Dow	Born 1/27/1879 Hancock, ME Died 8/1961 Hamburg, NY 1 wife, 4 children	Presidents: Harding, Coolidge, Hoover, Roosevelt, Truman, Eisenhower, Kennedy Prohibition in effect 1919-33 Great U.S. depression 1929-33 Television introduced in U.S. 1939 World War II 1941-45 Bell Labs creates first transistor 1947 Korean War 1950-53

PART 2

George—Growing Up and Going to Sea

210 years and eight generations after the first Dow landed in America, George W. Dow is born into a Maine seafaring family, and becomes a sea captain before he is 21.

GEORGE'S EARLY DAYS

WILLIAM AND NAOMI'S third child and first son, George Washington Dow, was born into the seafaring family in November 1847 in Tremont. The name George was not an ancestral Dow family name, but people and places were still commonly named Washington and George Washington in the post-revolutionary, mid-19th century. After all, it was less than 50 years since President Washington's death. (George's father William had been given the middle name Hamilton, presumably referencing Alexander Hamilton, who was a contemporary of William's father.)

Young George attended grade school at the McFarland Hill School, at the corner of Old County Road and what is now Route 1, just down the road from his home.

George W. Dow at eighteen

In 1857, Hancock had eight school districts and at least as many schools. Up until the late 1800's, however, students infrequently attended the schools. They were one-room affairs, heated by a wood stove or fireplace, and with the woods behind the school serving as the bathroom. Each child's family was expected to provide three-eighths of a cord of wood, two feet long, for the winter term.

It is unclear whether George went to high school, which would have meant commuting to Ellsworth, or started sailing with his father or other crews sailing out of Hancock. It was typical of 19th century seafaring families in Maine for the teenage sons who were interested to begin sailing with their fathers or on vessels captained by other relatives or acquaintances. Sons who became expert and sought to make seafaring a career, sometimes succeeded their fathers in mastering the same vessels.

In 1858, George's uncle Charles became captain of the new schooner *D. N. Richards*, a 99-ton, 74-foot-long vessel, built on Burying Island in Taunton Bay, between North Hancock and North Sullivan. She was built and owned by locals Lemuel Crabtree, M.E. Pettengill, and Elijah Stratton—all of Hancock— and sailed out of Hancock until 1861, when she was put under the command of another Hancock shipmaster, Herman Joy.

Later in life, Charles ran the Taunton River ferry between Hancock and Sullivan on the mainland. He died in 1888 in Hancock at age 74.

Although the first three Christian churches in Hancock were built between 1824 and 1867, it is unclear whether any of the three Hancock Dow families—including George—were members or attended. The religious fervor of past Dow generations had faded, despite the fairly stern Baptist faith that prevailed in Hancock. As a Hancock historian relates about the town—with application to the Dow family and to all of Maine, perhaps:

> *There were too many sea captains who were very worldly people and Maine was too much of a wilderness.*

As his grandfather, father, and three uncles before him, George Washington Dow became a merchant mariner early in his life, and was a master mariner, or ship's captain, by the time he was 21. For years, he sailed the world, especially to and from the Spanish Main—generally the coastal region surrounding the Caribbean, and reaching from Panama to the mouth of the Orinoco River in Venezuela.

Although he sailed for many shipping companies, he sailed more than 20 years on ships owned by John S. Emery & Company, with headquarters in Boston. Overall, he captained at least two barks and five schooners—and perhaps many more—before retiring in 1910.

BECOMING A SAILOR

LITTLE IS KNOWN about how young George was introduced to sailing and vessels, or how his interest and experience progressed from childhood to being named captain—as we shall see later—of the schooner *Stampede* in 1875 at age 28.

As a family new to Hancock, the Dows took their place among those longer-tenured families of Hancock that were oriented toward shipbuilding and sailing, rather than those devoted more toward farming and other local businesses and self-supporting endeavors. In establishing themselves in North Hancock, the Dows and other mariners became relatively prosperous contributors to the Town's population and evolving cultural mix. Shipbuilding and the merchant marine life, in particular, required a broader and less provincial outlook and orientation, dealing with people in other towns, territories, and even countries. The rewards, dangers, and required long voyages and absences all became parts of the normal lives of this group within Maine coastal communities like Hancock.

George grew up in his seafaring family during the heydays of Hancock shipbuilding and merchant sailing in the 1850's and 1860's. Although his father farmed, he also captained the *Fulcrum* from the time George was six, for at least eight years. And, uncle Charles had built, owned, and captained the *D.N. Richards* from the time George was nine. Besides William, Charles, and Samuel, another of George's uncles—Willis Dow, then still living in Mt. Desert—was also a captain for much of his adult life.

George's much younger brother Henry F. Dow (born in 1865) went to sea early on. At age 12 or 14, he was a cabin boy but unexpectedly changed ships and ended up traveling to England, South Africa, and the Pacific, arriving back home months later. Following years at sea, he went on to work as a gardener in Parsippany, New Jersey, his wife having agreed to marry him on the condition that he forego seafaring.

There have been rumors in the family that George did, in fact, sail frequently—and perhaps far and wide—with his father and/ or his uncles and others, instead of attending or completing high school. But, only rumors they are, and they are not substantiated or detailed by any written or otherwise convincing records.

All the same, school attendance was, not to say "optional," but often not strictly required or adhered to, creating more opportunities for school-age boys to serve as crew members and learn many aspects of seafaring, both locally and on regional or longer voyages.

It is certain that George relished sailing and became good at it quickly and early on, even though we are frustrated by an absence of any record of his early life's experiences, including his introduction and devotion to sailing. Did George sail with his father, uncles, and on other locally-owned vessels? Which ones, where to, and what was his role? And, did his exposure to local Hancock ship builders and owners—Elijah Stratton and the Emerys of Sullivan, for example—include early "on-deck" experiences that served to hone his skills, prove his abilities, and engender respect and loyalty as his Boston-based career developed?

All but two of George's nine siblings spent most or all of their lives Down East and in local work and activities. And, the two who did not, moved to Boston and did not sail. But, for George, there is no record of his devoting significant time and career attention to anything other than sailing—including farming or as an employee of local manufacturers or retail businesses.

A WIFE

ABOUT TWO YEARS after becoming a master, George married Jennie Bush on July 13, 1870, in Hancock, with Robert Cole officiating at the church.

Johanna Wilhelmina Bush, in America always known as Jennie, was born in Oldenburg, Germany, in April of 1847 and made the voyage to America as a very young girl. She was her parents' seventh child and fifth daughter.

Jennie Bush's father, Dr. Ernest O. Bush, probably emigrated from Oldenburg with three children, including Jennie, in Oc-

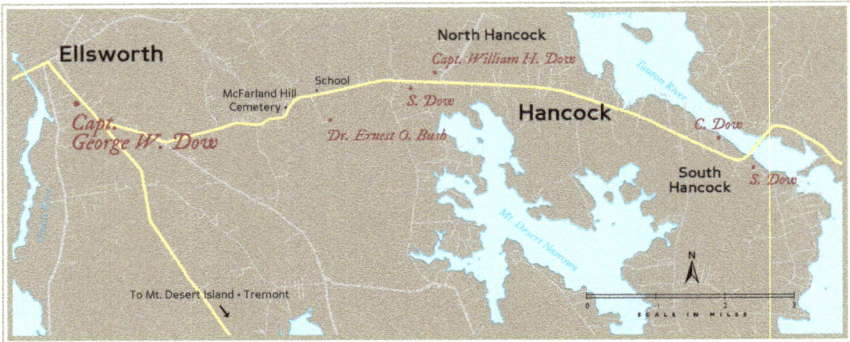

Captain Dow grows up in North Hancock, marries Jennie Bush, a doctor's daughter from across the street, and lives in nearby Ellsworth for 15 years.

tober of 1854, at age 56. He built a house sometime after 1860 on a farm just south of the County Road (now Route 1) in North Hancock and not far from the W. H. Dow house where George lived. Nine more Bush children came from Germany by 1862 for a total of 12. There was no sign of the Doctor having a wife in America, and his household included Thomas Ulfers, who also was brought from Germany during this time and lived with the Bush family. Ulfers was a mariner and never married. Dr. Bush was naturalized as an American citizen in April of 1868.

There is another, different story of how the Bush family arrived in America and Maine, although the two versions do not diverge significantly from the general timing and outcome of their arrival in Hancock:

Dr. Bush left his native Germany abruptly in the spring of 1858. At the time, German laws prohibited the sale of woolen clothes to the lower classes, but Dr. Bush, who specialized in lung troubles, insisted that the warm clothing was needed to maintain the health of the working class in Oldenburg. This angered the authorities there, and they retaliated by canceling his license to practice medicine. Approaching 60 years of age, and with his livelihood threatened and a family to support, Dr. Bush decided to seek new opportunities in America.

Jennie Bush Dow's German language bible. The "Dr. Martin Luthers" volume was printed in Hanover, Germany, in 1838, and signed by "Johanna Wilhelmine Bushe" in 1857, when she was 10 years old.

Having little money, the Doctor accepted an offer of free passage to the United States by an American sea captain who was ready to sail and had heard the Doctor's story. Bush quickly got his wife and 12 children aboard, taking a large tent and some household goods. We have no evidence, or even stories, of the captain's or the ship's identities.

The passage was stormy, and Mrs. Bush took sick and died early in the voyage. Another woman passenger, a widow with a small boy, also died, and Dr. Bush "adopted" the orphan— possibly Thomas Ulfers, although he would have been well into his 20's at the time.

Arriving in Maine with few belongings and no home or job— and speaking only German—Dr. Bush and his family at first lived in the tent pitched on the shore at South Hancock.

What is certain, is that he learned English, staked out his farm and built a house just south of the J. H. McFarland homestead in North Hancock, and built a successful career caring for the medical needs of both humans and animals in the area. Sometimes on the road for days at a time, his territory covered most of Hancock and western Washington counties.

Dr. Bush created a makeshift quarantine in a separate wing of his house, bringing tuberculosis patients to his farm to recuperate. In those days, TB was thought to be caused by a cold and wet climate, and people did not believe it to be contagious. Isolated on the Bush farm, patients were given special diets and spent long hours resting in bed. Dr. Bush also farmed his land in Hancock.

By 1872, Dr. Bush had the means to pay off the $140 mortgage loan on his 97-acre property, the note being held by lender Arthur Drinkwater of Ellsworth.

FAMILY IN ELLSWORTH

IN AUGUST OF 1871, a year after George and Jennie were married, they moved to Ellsworth and into a house they purchased at the corner of Washington Street and High Street (the "Ellsworth-Mt. Desert" road), not three-quarters of a mile from the Ellsworth post office. The Captain bought the house for $500 cash from William H. Black, and would live there for the next 15 years—at least when he was not at sea. Ellsworth was the center of Hancock County, larger than the town of Hancock, and only about five miles west along County Road from the William Dow and Ernest Bush houses where Captain George and Jennie had grown up.

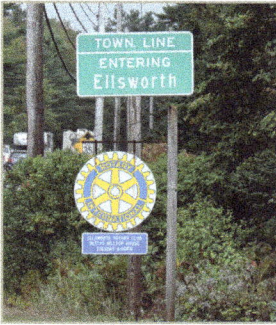

Before moving to Ellsworth, George and Jennie lived at one of their parents' houses, both of which were undoubtedly crowded and not ideal for newlyweds. For example, in 1870, George and at least seven of his siblings were still living in the William Dow house in North Hancock.

Their first child, son Orville Howard Dow, was born in 1871 in North Hancock, at either the Dow or Bush house. Orville was the first of four children George and Jennie were to have, with two of them dying at the young age of four.

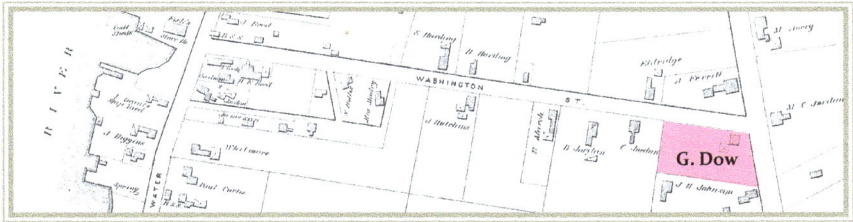

From 1871, Captain Dow and Jennie live in Ellsworth on a corner lot along the Ellsworth-Mt. Desert Road.

However he spent his time as a teenager and young adult—as a student, a sailor, or on other things—he apparently did well. For, by the time he was 24, he had married Jennie in 1870, bought a house for cash in Ellsworth in 1871, and they had their first child Orville in 1871, all indicating a certain level of prosperity. There is evidence of an entrepreneurial side later in his life, but little evidence of any business involvement as a teenager or young adult. And, there is no history of wealth in the family before him, or of any inheritance, either from his father (to his 10 children) or Jennie's father (to his 12 children).

The captain's large plot in an 1870's residential area is now a strip mall on a busy highway.

A Career as a Captain

N O INDICATION HAS BEEN FOUND as to which vessels he captained during the first seven years of his career as an adult, from 1868 to 1875. He certainly could have taken over intermittently as captain on a number of locally-built schooners or other vessels when their owners were 'between captains,' or when captains were sick or called away temporarily. The seven years could have gone by rapidly, with fewer than a dozen long voyages. But, we do not know, and there are other possibilities.

Research suggests a number of vessels that could be candidates for Captain Dow's early career as a captain, but every such case uncovered so far has proven to be questionable or a dead end.

The existence of another, contemporaneous Captain George W. Dow from Maine—dubbed the "wrong Captain Dow" by our family—has resulted in some mistaken leads. Born in 1834 in Searsport, Maine, and only 13 years older than our Captain Dow, the Wrong One therefore had an overlapping career, and has made research more complex and confusing. But, the Wrong GWD owned and captained vessels based out of the Bucksport and Belfast area along the Penobscot River, sailed for different vessel owners (especially the Brookmans of New York), and ventured from a variety of East Coast ports, including Providence, Rhode Island, and New York, as well as Boston.

The library at Mystic Seaport in Mystic, Connecticut, has an extensive trove of artifacts from the Wrong George W. Dow that include port charges for passage, piloting and towing, supplies, and repairs; cargo receipts; charter documents; crew lists; and bills of lading, among many other things. All these items date from March 1847—the year of our George W. Dow's birth—to 1863, the year our GWD turned 16 years old. So, the many vessels and ports of call up and down the East Coast, Latin America, and Europe that are cited do not relate to our Captain.

Similarly, the brig *Webster Kelly* and schooners *Francis Newton* and *N.R. Hagan* are all attributable to the Wrong Dow, prior to his becoming Master of the brig *Wenonah* in 1857. He remained on the *Wenonah* for at least four years, and then on the *Albatross* until 1865, when he took command of the brig *Alberti* on which he served for six years until 1871. (Records also indicate a vessel *Catherine Ewan*, captained and part-owned by a George Dow in 1858-59.) Our George W. Dow was only 18 years old in 1865, thus, too young for all of these vessels.

The schooner *Nora* is listed with a Captain Geo. Dow from 1869 to 1875, which matches a gap in the sailing record of our Captain. However, *Nora* was built in Isleborough, with home ports successively including Camden and Belfast, in the heart of 'Wrong Dow' territory. And, there is no mention of the *Nora* in any reference relating to our man in Hancock or Ellsworth.

The bark *Shamrock*, built in Belfast, was captained in 1872 and 1873 by a George W. Dow. But, it shared the same owner—H.D. and J.U. Brookman—as other vessels captained by the Wrong George W. Dow. So, this is unlikely to have been our Captain Dow.

In any case, by the mid-1870's, Captain George W. Dow had become a well-known and popular master along the Atlantic coast and Spanish Main. He was also respected for his seamanship. And, he was not yet 30.

THE *STAMPEDE*

IN 1875, George signed on as master of the schooner *Stampede* out of Boston, and sailed her for the next seven years. At 145 tons and 95 feet by 26 feet by 9 feet, *Stampede* was built in Hancock in 1861, was owned by the original captain, Elijah Stratton, and others, and was based in Boston as her home port. Captain Dow had an ownership interest until 1877, when at least half the ownership changed hands for $6,000, and Calvin G. Peck became the *Stampede*'s principal owner. (But, even two years later in 1879, Hancock residents Alonzo Abbott and the estate of Calvin Berry still owned an eighth and a sixteenth share of *Stampede*, respectively.)

The *Stampede* had sailed the Americas during the 14 years before George Dow became her master, including under Captain Stratton from Hancock. These routes continued under Captain Dow. In November 1875, she sailed from Boston to Mobile, Alabama, to Port au Prince, Haiti, and then back up to Boston, arriving in April of the following year. The ship's mate—T.C. Moon and also from Hancock—wrote an article about Captain Dow on this trip, published in *The Ellsworth American* newspaper 50 years later. The narrative sheds light on the Captain's steady demeanor, instincts, and sailing skills at age 28. Moon writes:

I was captain of the schooner Redondo of Ellsworth during the summer and fall of 1875. In November I shipped as mate on the schooner Stampede. Captain George Dow was in command. We sailed from Boston the day after Thanksgiving.

The day we sailed, the captain said he had ordered a new log, but it must have been overlooked. But, he added, "I don't need a log, for I have sailed this schooner several years, and I can judge her rate of sailing within two or three miles every twenty-four hours, so you can make your record in the log book, and then every day when we take the observation of the sun, we can make corrections if any are needed."

After a fair passage to Mobile, we loaded the lumber. We had a deck load, and the deck of the schooner was only three inches out of water, but that was the regular load line for a Maine schooner.

A few days after we sailed from Mobile, we ran into a gale and had rain squalls all the time. For seven days we never saw the sun to take an observation. The captain had never had the experience before—no observation and no log to guide him.

It was my watch on deck from 8 to noon, on the seventh day.

At 6 p.m. it was still raining. The captain (George Dow) ordered the flying jib taken in and furled, and the schooner (Stampede) brought by the wind with the jib to windward. The wheel was put hard down and lashed. The schooner lay nearly head to the sea on the port tack. One man was on lookout and one at the pump. It was my watch below from 6 to 8 p.m. The captain was up and down watching the weather. The barometer was rising. He said it would clear off after midnight.

About 7:30, I was sitting in the cabin waiting to go on deck at 8 o'clock, when the captain came down, went to his stateroom and got his pipe. He stood in the cabin filling his pipe. He stood with his feet wide apart to steady himself, as the schooner was rolling badly. He began to tell a story. The cook had come in, and he sat beside me to hear the captain, who could tell a good story.

All at once the man on lookout shouted, "Breakers! All hands on deck!" The captain dropped his pipe and ran up the after steps to the wheel. The cook and I ran up the forward steps to the deck. We could hear the roar of the surf on the reef. The captain shouted, "Wear ship; lower the main peak!" He rolled the wheel hard up. I gave the order to lower the main peak, and started for the peak downhaul.

The captain shouted, "Hold on the main peak, and every man look out for that sea!" I looked forward and I saw a sea like a small mountain coming. Up went the bow of the schooner, until I thought she was standing on her stern, than down went her bow until the jib boom and captain were under water, but up she came. Then another sea came over her, then the third, not quite so heavy. These seas came a little on the lee box, and that made stern way on the schooner and, acting on the rudder, turned the schooner so she went in stays and filed away on the starboard tack. That saved the schooner for if we had worn ship, it would have taken so long we would have gone ashore, and the schooner would never have been heard of.

As soon as we had steerage way, the captain ordered me to get the deep-sea lead, and see how much water we had under us. I got the lead and ordered two men to take it to the fore chains, and when ready to heave, to let me know. As soon as the man was ready, the captain luffed the schooner into the wind so as to stop her headway, and then gave the order to heave the lead. I watched the line run through my hand until it stopped at twelve fathoms. It took three men to haul in the lead. The captain gave the schooner a hard pull and drove her all she could go. In twenty minutes we hove the lead again, and could not reach bottom after thirty fathoms had run out. We could not hear the roar of the breaker any more. The breakers we had heard were on a coral reef out some three or four miles from an island, and if we had not hove in when we did, we should have run head on the reef. But our time had not come, so we escaped.

Two days after we were nearly wrecked, we arrived in Port au Prince, and discharged the deckload as soon as possible. Before it was all discharged, the leak stopped, so we knew that the leak was near the top. When the cargo was all out, I found the leak and stopped the place where the oakum had worked out of the seams. We loaded with logwood for Boston, where we arrived in April, 1876.

Captain Dow was one of the best ship masters that the State of Maine had produced. I shall never forget that night so near the breakers and 'Davy Jones locker.'

Seven years later, in February of 1882, the crew of the *Stampede* abandoned ship off Cape Fear, North Carolina, during a night storm on a trip from Jacksonville, Florida, to New York, with a cargo of Southern lumber. A day later, the crew was picked up by the Austrian bark Melchior Vidulich, which arrived in Boston on February 13, having sailed from Sagua la Grande, Cuba. The *Stampede's* First Officer F. C. Benthlen, native of Denmark, was lost and one seaman was seriously injured, but the rest of the crew survived. The *Stampede* was a complete loss, and it is not clear if Captain Dow was aboard or had already moved on from the *Stampede*.

Despite commuting to Boston and spending long months at sea, in 1877 Captain Dow and Jennie had a daughter, Georgie Wilhelmina Dow, born in Hancock. Georgie was to live only four years, dying—possibly from scarlet fever—in 1881. She is buried in Hancock's McFarland Hill Cemetery. Some fifty years later, Jennie left to her granddaughter, Mary Elizabeth Dow, a small hand fan that had belonged to daughter Georgie. The note attached indicated: "That velvet fan was my dear little daughter's, the ornamentations are fish scales." The fan was no doubt brought back by the Captain from somewhere far off.

Two years later, on January 27, 1879, their second son, Richard Ernest Dow, was born in Hancock. And, the next year, the Dow family headcount in Ellsworth grew to six, with the birth of Ellery Channing Dow. Like his sister Georgie, however, Ellery was to live only four years, dying in 1884.

In 1882, the Maine Shore Line Railroad Company planned to extend its tracks 39 miles from the town of Brewer through Ellsworth and Washington Junction and on to McNeil Point in South Hancock, where passengers could board the steamer ferries to cross the six miles of water across Frenchman's Bay and arrive at the town pier in Bar Harbor on Mt. Desert Island. In May of 1883, Captain Dow's father William agreed to allow the railroad to cut across his land south of County Highway with a right of way four rods (66 feet) wide, for which the railroad paid him $50.

With financing from the Maine Central Railroad, the largest and premier railroad line in New England at the time, the extension was built and then opened with the Mt. Desert Limited (later named the Bar Harbor Express). From around the turn of the century until 1931, this train allowed summer vacationers from Washington, D.C., Philadelphia, and New York to travel

The Bar Harbor Express near Ellsworth, Maine

in luxury and directly to the Mt. Desert resorts. The line was so important to the Maine Central that the company's President would ride the route just prior to each summer season, to ensure the service was first rate and the ride so smooth as not to spill coffee or champagne. Explosive growth in automobile travel, and then in travel by air, took its toll on railroads across the country, and the Hancock/Mt. Desert route was truncated back to Ellsworth in 1931, back to Bangor in 1957, and finally abandoned altogether a few years after that. ⚓

PART 3

Family and Seafaring in Melrose

*Building his career as an ocean-going master,
Captain Dow moves his family from Maine
to his home port of Boston.*

THE *GEM*

I N 1884, the Captain became master of the bark *GEM*, which was owned by John S. Emery & Co., sailing out of Boston. Although the Emery company was Boston-based, the Emery family was from Sullivan Township, Maine—just across the Taunton River from Hancock. As a result, the Dows and Emerys knew of each other well. And, it is reasonable to assume that sometime after leaving the *Stampede*, the Captain approached John or Daniel Emery at their State Street headquarters in the Port of Boston, seeking a new vessel to captain.

The *GEM* was built in 1861 and overhauled in 1881. She displaced 545 tons and was 144 feet long, with a 31-foot beam and 15 foot draft. She had two decks. Captain Dow stayed aboard her from 1884 until 1886. Seven years later, in 1893, *GEM* was lost on the rocks near San Francisco.

There was a group of vessels directly attributable to the Wrong Captain Dow, including *Kolon, Melona M. Knowles, Tally Ho,* and *Rebecca Crowell.* And, a few others must have been under his command, because they otherwise conflicted with our Captain Dow's known assignments on other vessels during the same years.

The brig *Lizzie Zittlosen,* built in Millbridge and captained by a George W. Dow in 1872-73, and from 1875 to 1886, must have been a mainstay for the Wrong Captain. Meanwhile, our Captain Dow was occupied on the *Stampede* and *GEM,* from 1875 to 1882, and 1884 to 1886, respectively.

And, the same for the schooner *M.C. Niosleil,* according to a single crew list reference and sailing from Boston to Santa Cruz, West Indies, in 1880, with a 33-year-old, 5' 10" "Geo. W. Dow" as its captain. His birthplace and place of residence is cited as "Maine." No other reference to this vessel or Dow affiliation could be found. Although it could have been a one-off voyage by our Captain Dow, any greater commitment would have interfered and conflicted with his 1875-82 stint as master of the *Stampede.*

The schooner *M.C. Moseley,* sailing from Boston during 1881-84 conflicts with our Captain Dow being on the *Stampede.* And, the half-brig *Ned White* was captained out of Belfast by a Captain Dow in 1885-86, which was in conflict with our Captain's years on the *GEM.*

Settling in Melrose

I N 1886, two years after signing on to the *GEM*, his first
Emery vessel, the captain moved his family from Ellsworth to the Boston suburb of Melrose, about ten miles from
Boston harbor, Boston having been his home port for many
years. (Melrose was then a part of Charlestown called "Malden
North End.") He and Jennie were to live at 345 Upham Street
in Melrose until his death in 1919, and hers in 1931.

The move to Melrose represents the engagement of the Dow
family line with urban American society, after nearly 250
years and nine generations in rural New England. This reflects
the country's continuing, rapid population growth westward
from the New England colonies, and the industrialization of
the country that was accelerating urbanization. The port of
Boston had become the hub for Captain Dow and his family,

345 Upham Street, Melrose, Massachusetts, as it looks now,
130 years after the Captain and Jennie moved In.

from which his descendants would eventually radiate across the country.

For many years after moving to Melrose, however, the Captain and Jennie kept close ties to family members and old acquaintances in the Hancock-Ellsworth area.

THE *ALBERT L. BUTLER*

F OLLOWING *GEM*, the Captain signed onto the three-masted schooner *Albert L. Butler* for about five years, from 1886 to 1891. The *Butler* had just been overhauled at Thomaston, Maine, where she had been built by Walker Dunn & Co. in 1869. She was owned by Emery, and sailed from Boston. She was 327 tons and 120 feet long, with a 30-foot beam, and drew 15 feet of water—and had two decks. Perhaps his first voyage on the *Butler* was a trip in November 1886, making a stop in Charleston, South Carolina, on his way from Boston to Kingston, Jamaica.

Seven years after Captain Dow left the *Butler*, she was wrecked at Peaked Hill Bars at Provincetown during the infamous Portland Gale on November 27, 1898, along with at least 140 other major vessels lost between Cape Cod and Portland, Maine. Five *Butler* crew were saved, three others were lost, and the schooner was a total loss.

The Captain's two sons were fifteen and seven years old at the time of the move to Melrose, and were to progress through the Melrose public school system. Oldest son Orville graduated about 1889 from Melrose High School. He was

For five years, Captain Dow is master of the *Abert L. Butler* shown here as a wreck in 1898, seven years after Captain Dow left its command.

> *... prominent in school affairs ... and was highly regarded by his teachers and his school associates. He was a man of fine character and in the broader school of life had contracted many friendships.*

During the 1880's, the Captain's family took in a nephew, Girard Graves, when Girard moved to Boston from Hancock to seek work. Girard probably lived in the Captain's home in Melrose until his marriage in 1893. Girard was born in Hancock on January 30, 1870, to Jennie's sister Ernestine Bush and her husband (perhaps) Frank Graves. There were Graves family houses on both sides of William Dow's house in North Hancock. With his parents living apart, Girard lived with his grandfather Bush's family in Hancock until moving to Boston.

THE AUBURNDALE

I N 1891, Captain Dow became Master of the three-masted bark *Auburndale*, the largest vessel he had captained, and also owned by the Emery company. The *Auburndale* was built in Millbridge, Maine, in 1880, sailed from Boston, weighed 574 tons, was 150 feet by 33 feet, drew 17 feet, and had two decks. Tonnage increased to 630 tons in 1895, then to 664 tons in 1898.

The *Auburndale* was to be the Captain's longest command, lasting nearly 15 years, from 1891 to 1905. Captain Dow owned a 4/64th share of the *Auburndale*, with various members of the Emery family owning a total of nearly 30% (Daniel S. Emery owned 9/64th, John S. owned 8/64th, Prudence S. 1/64th, and Lydia S. 1/64th).

Although the *Auburndale*'s log is lost, we do know that she traveled the seas beyond the Spanish Main, as First Mate Libby says he "crossed the Atlantic many times on the *Auburndale*." And, a letter from Peter Strickland relates his plans for his trip home from Liverpool, England, on the bark *Auburndale*, in September of 1905.

On perhaps his first voyage aboard the *Auburndale* in 1891, The Captain sailed to the Caribbean, and returned from Cienfuegos, Cuba, to Boston on June 3 of that year. That November, they sailed for Cape Town, South Africa, with a cargo including 100 reels of "barb wire," ladders, farm implements, tools, wheelbarrows, and hardware.

From tax and port records over the following decade and a

Captain Dow enjoys his longest command—14 years—
on the three-masted bark *Auburndale*, running cargoes to and from the
Spanish Main and Europe.

half, we catch glimpses of the *Auburndale* and Captain Dow's comings and goings at ports including Bath, Boston, New York, Washington D.C., Charleston, Cienfuegos (Cuba), Rosario and Buenos Aires (Argentina), and Trinidad (British West Indies). One trip in 1894 from Rosario consisted of 10,000 dry hides.

On December 22, 1898, the *Auburndale*, loaded with salt from Buenos Aires, Argentina, ran aground during a thick fog a mile and a half off the Atlantic coast, south southwest of Barnegat Light on New Jersey's outer banks. In high surf and stormy weather, the local rescue crews from the Harvey Cedars, Ship Bottom and Loveladies Island stations arrived and had to take two gun shot tries at shooting a line onto the bark and rigging up a breeches buoy to take the men off. After four of the crew made it across to the lifeboat and then to shore, the wind shifted and the Captain and rest of the crew decided to stay aboard. The rescue crew from Harvey Cedars stayed by the stranded vessel, while the other two boats returned to their stations. At midnight, the weather worsened, so three more of the crew went across, leaving Captain Dow and three others still on board, where they decided to wait for daylight.

At about 9:00 am, the wrecking tug *North America* arrived from Philadelphia, but could not pull the *Auburndale* off her grounding. They then decided to dump 100 tons of salt and try again. The maneuver worked, and the tug hauled her off and towed her into New York harbor, leaking slightly but not otherwise damaged. She went to Erie Basin in Brooklyn to be dry docked for caulking. The *Auburndale*'s crewmembers that had gone ashore in the breeches buoy were fed and lodged at the Harvey Cedars lifeboat stations for two days.

In 1898, a Captain Dow was listed for the schooner *Harold C. Beacher,* out of Boston, but this would have been right in the middle of our relative's long stint on the *Auburndale.*

A fine silk top hat, made by Ecolasse in Paris, and presented to the captain by the Government of Cuba, probably while master of the *Auburndale* in the 1890's.

Beginning in 1859, the American Seamen's Friend Society placed loan libraries of books on board American vessels sailing from Boston and New York, and Captain Dow took full advantage on the *Auburndale.* Each "library" consisted of some 40 volumes placed in a wooden case with a hinged door that resembled a small bookcase and could be locked. They were placed aboard by the "Ship's Visitor," who worked the waterfronts. Several communications during the 1890's between the Captain and the Society regarding borrowed books and the *Sailor's Magazine and Seamen's Friend* indicate that Captain Dow— and presumably his crews—valued the program. He states that the volumes were

> *Read and re-read by myself and many others, and has helped to pass away many lonesome hours, for which I am very thankful; but as I have lent the books out to different ones, in some instances I have failed to get them back, forgetting about them myself and those that had them forgot to return them; some perhaps purposely;*

there are a few of the books missing, but will gladly return what I have, whether I get any more or not.

Over the 70 years from 1859 to 1930, the Society placed more than a million books into the hands or mariners at sea.

As a gift from one of his loyal crews, most likely of the *Auburndale*, Captain Dow acquired a West Indian planter's chair, known also as a "lazy man's chair." This is a large chair, leaning back at a good angle, with double wooden slats for arms. The lower slat on each side swivels out to the front, crossing to form a stand on which to rest one's legs, sore from the day's planting and horseback work. The chair still remains with the Dow (Turner) family. Luckily, Captain Dow left it at home in Melrose years later when he went off on the *Thomas W. Lawson.*

The caribbean planter's chair—with long swivel arms—given to Captain Dow by one of his grateful crews more than a century ago.

MELROSE HOME LIFE

O N DECEMBER 8, 1891, just after having taken charge of the *Auburndale*, Captain Dow was elected to the Boston Marine Society. This society for sea captains was founded by a group of Boston captains in 1754, to establish training programs for mariners. It also made payments to poor families of captains lost at sea. It was in its hay-day in the 1890's, with its membership peaking at 475 in 1893. The society still exists at the Charlestown Navy Yard in Boston, and its membership is growing again, as recreational sailors in the Boston area affiliate with it.

A distant cousin of Captain Dow (actually his 8th cousin), Captain Millard G. Dow of Searsport, Maine, was elected into the BMS in 1893, but the membership was rescinded several months later for "non-payment of membership fee." Millard, born in 1859, captained many vessels, including the *Rebecca Crowell*, and the *Marion Manson*. He was the son of our previously-described "wrong" Captain George W. Dow, who was born in 1834 and sailed the world during the same decades as our ancestral Captain George W. Dow, from the 1860's into the 1890's. He commanded the brig *Wenonah*, of Bucksport, which carried coal, lead, flour, molasses, and other foodstuffs to ports in the U.S., West Indies, Canary Islands, and to Cadiz, Spain.

Meanwhile, on the home front, Girard Graves married Rebecca Lewis Jennings Pratt in Boston, in 1893. By 1900, Girard, Rebecca and their 6-year-old daughter Mildred were living with Rebecca's parents in Boston. Another female baby lived only three months in 1896, but a son, Lewis, was born in 1902, and another daughter, Harriet, in 1906. Over the next few years at least, Girard worked

In 1891, Captain Dow was elected to the Boston Marine Society

as a salesman, taking orders throughout southern New England for silverware, paper boxes, and other items.

Captain Dow's father William passed away at age 74 on September 25, 1894, while in Gouldsboro, Maine, just east of Hancock. He may have been visiting his daughters Martha or Julia, who both lived in Gouldsboro. In his later years, William used to tell his grandchildren—presumably Orville, Richard, and perhaps Girard Graves—stories of his old-time ancestors and various wars, Indian fights, privations, massacres, scalpings, and bravery. He would admonish them to pass on these tales and names to their own future children and grand children. But, alas, this was not heeded.

Less than two years later, the Captain's mother Naomi died in Hancock on June 21, 1896. Both William and Naomi are buried at McFarland Hill Cemetery in Hancock, just west of their long-time home.

In Melrose, a local club, Melrose Sons and Daughters of Maine, was formed in January of 1895, to promote "social intercourse among its members." Eligibility for membership was open to "natives of Maine above the age of eighteen years and residing in Melrose, as also the wife or husband of such natives so residing." In 1902, the membership numbered 175. It is unclear whether any of the George W. Dow family were members, although they were eligible.

The Dow family was comfortable and prospered in Melrose. In 1891, the Captain and Jennie had a formal portrait photograph taken of 12-year-old son Richard—and perhaps one of older son

The Captain's 12-year-old son Richard in 1891,
and 17-year-old Richard in 1896.

Orville at the same time, as well—by the local, Emerson Place professional photographer Selee. (Frank Selee, a member of the entrepreneurial Selee family in Melrose, was a Hall of Fame baseball manager, winning nine pennants with the Boston Beaneaters and Chicago Cubs (previously the Orphans), between 1890 and 1905.)

Five years later, in 1896, another "cabinet photograph" was made of then 17-year-old Richard, this time by the "European Photographer" Carl Horner on Winter Street in Boston. This photo, like the earlier one, shows young Richard in coat and tie. Coincidently, and demonstrating the rising role of baseball as the National Pastime, Horner, a Swedish portrait specialist who set up shop in Boston in the 1880's, became the most famous producer of of baseball player portraits in the 1890's and into the

20th Century. His images were used on many of the early baseball cards—initially cigarette pack premiums—including the Honus Wagner card, baseball's most famous card ever, one of which sold at auction in 2013 for $2.1 million.

Son Richard was, with his older brother Orville, educated in the Melrose public schools from 1886 onward. Known to the locals as "Dicky Dow," he was "one of the most popular Melrose boys...especially noted as a cornet player." Richard's daughter believed that he never graduated from high school, because his father (the Captain) took him on voyages to England, Africa, and elsewhere, presumably on the *Auburndale*. But, no supportive documentation or even family stories seem to exist.

In any case, Richard attended the Massachusetts Institute of Technology (MIT) from 1897 to 1901, receiving a bachelor's degree in chemistry. The college was located in the Back Bay neighborhood of Boston and known as "Technology" or "Boston Tech" in those days. Upon graduation, Richard took a job with the Massachusetts State Board of Health in Boston.

During his college-year summers, Richard earned money for school playing his cornet in resorts up through Maine. And, locally in Melrose, he organized a ten-member orchestra—known as "Dow's Orchestra"—which he led and managed at least through 1902, a year after his graduation. Playing the cornet at home became a daily part of his life for the next half century.

Captain Dow's wife Jennie had a "real German temper." In 1906 or 1907, son Richard met his future girlfriend and wife Annie Dinnie at a horse-drawn bus stop where Annie caught the bus to

Captain Dow (standing), Jennie, and the Captain's younger
brother Prentiss and nephew George, ca. 1905

work teaching school each day. She was born in 1879 in Quincy, to a granite polisher and his wife, both from Aberdeenshire, Scotland. Living in nearby Quincy, she was a "remarkable school marm." Later, when Richard brought Annie home and announced they planned to marry, Jennie threw an iron stove handle across the room at the fiancé. Jennie was against the marriage, and the two women never really had a close relationship. It is said that Jennie had another woman in mind for Richard to marry. There are, however, postcards to Jennie sent by Annie over the next few years that convey no apparent antagonism.

In addition to his career as a sea captain, Captain Dow was a partner in a business dealing with farm implements, located in Ellsworth and in partnership with brother in law and local Hancock businessman George W. Young. Young was married to the Captain's younger sister Rose Ellen Dow, and they lived in the Balm of Gideon Inn (well before it burned down in the 1930's or early 1940's). Young had a variety of retail businesses in Hancock County, including a warehouse in Ellsworth. He represented the harvesting machinery company Adriance, Platt & Co., of Poughkeepsie, New York, from about 1885.

George Young had taken on Captain Dow as a partner, perhaps only a financial one. The partnership was a sideline and a long way from home for the Captain. The firm, Young & Dow, advertised in the *Ellsworth American* their meshing and wood-sawing machines, gasoline engines, and horse powers, carriages, and harnesses: "Everything that a farmer needs." In October 1905, however, the Captain withdrew from the business. The story in the Ellsworth paper indicated:

> *The firm of Young & Dow—dealers in agricultural imple-ments—has been dissolved. The business will be continued by Mr. Young in the basement of the old Lord's hall building on Main Street. Captain Dow left town Monday, for Mel-rose, Mass. He has not decided whether he will go into busi-ness again, or go back to his old calling of going to sea.*

He chose the latter.

Whether this was a falling out between the Captain and George Young is not known. Probably not, however, as the Captain and his sister Rose Young remained close. A postcard from Rose in Hancock to the Captain in Melrose in 1908 says:

> *Dear Geo.*
> *Have sent today Oct. 14th 1 bbl. Of potatoes by freight.*
> *Please let us no when received. All well.*
> *—R.E.Y.*

Withdrawing from the Ellsworth partnership with Young may have ended Captain Dow's last commercial and financial activity in Maine, and the Captain's business career reflects broader changes that were taking place in Maine at the beginning of the 20th century.

The optimism and opportunity that characterized Maine through the late 18th and 19th centuries had peaked, and a decline in economic activity and growth had set in, driving future generations to leave the state in search of greener pastures. (Peter Merrill points out that this is "A questionable metaphor in this case, since it is hard to be 'greener' than Maine, except with respect to the color of money.")

Captain Dow's long stint as master of the *Auburndale* had come to an end before 1907. (In July of 1908, the *Auburndale* sailed from Turk's Island for Portland, Oregon, with a cargo of salt and was never heard of again. It is believed that she went down off Cape Hatteras during the West Indies hurricane that swept up the east coast that month.)

In 1907, son Orville Dow was a 36-year-old pharmacist in East Boston. He had married Hazel Anita Lorde and they had a son, George Orville, in Boston in 1902, and a daughter, Josephine, born in 1907, also in Boston. 28-year-old son Richard was working as Assistant Chief Chemist at the Massachusetts State Board of Health, in Boston.

At that time, the worlds of shipping and commerce were changing radically and rapidly, and this maelstrom was about to change the course of Captain Dow's life. ⚓

PART 4

The Lawson *and its Atlantic Crossing*

*60 years old and with four decades
of commanding vessels under his belt,
Captain George W. Dow
takes on an iconic schooner and encounters
the challenge of his life.*

THE SHIP

SAIL'S LAST GASP

A T THE END of the 19th century, steel ships and steam power were becoming the rule on the seas. Steam power was more reliable and controllable than wind, allowed for larger ships and cargoes, and required only a fraction of the number of sailors that large sailing ships needed. However, some ship-yards continued to build larger and more efficient sailing ships, not recognizing or yielding to the inherent superiority of steam over wind, or to the notion that commercial sailing was a doomed technology. And, although square-rigged ships generally had ruled the world's oceans, schooners with their rigging efficiencies had become the rig of choice for plying the east coast of the United States during the 1800's.

After the end of the Civil War in 1865, the industrial revolution shifted American attention and capital from maritime to domestic development, railroads and westward expansion. As a result, deep-water shipping declined temporarily, while demand for coastal bulk cargo transportation grew rapidly. The fleet of "coasters" expanded to fill this demand.

Maine was an important source of natural resources required for the booming building industries down the East Coast. These cargoes included lumber, lime, granite, ice, hay, and coal. Over months and years, boats would switch among cargoes, according to prices, availability, or conditions of the boats. Lumber cargoes were popular, because they made the boat practically unsinkable. At the other end of the spectrum, there were many stories of vessels loaded with granite sinking "like stones." And, lime—used for making mortar for laying bricks—caught fire when wet, requiring great efforts to seal the casks and holds.

It was not uncommon to see 250 sailing vessels in port at Bangor, Maine, for example. And, Maine shipyards built many of the schooners used elsewhere in the world, accounting for virtually all the much larger schooners launched around 1900. At the turn of the century, "Maine still had forests, slipways and know how."

"A boat's reputation could be based on its speed and handiness, exceptional or miserable accommodations, good or notorious captain, seaworthiness or pay." Some boats were owned by the captain and investors, who often were local folks but expected a good return on their share. A coaster sailing between mid-coast Maine and Boston or New York made eight to 12 trips a year.

THE BIG COASTAL SCHOONERS

S CHOONERS—that is, vessels with only fore-and-aft rigging and at least two masts—had been built and used in the North Sea since the early 1600's. The word *schooner* may have been first used in 1713, when a new ship was launched at Andrew Robinson's shipyard in Gloucester, Massachusetts. When the vessel entered the water, an observer remarked "Oh, how she schoons!" Robinson is said to have replied, "A schooner let her be."

The schooner fore-and-aft rigging is aerodynamically more efficient than square rigging, requires less sail and smaller crews, and is therefore faster and cheaper, especially in the face of the shifting and tricky coastal winds. The sails can be "drawn close in to the hum, parallel to the ship's length, and the bellying canvas then formed an airfoil with its low pressure side pulling the ship along" more directly into the wind than is possible with square sails. As a result of their speed and efficiency—and of growing demand for materials down the coast—larger and larger schooners

In September 1906, the *Lawson* is among five schooners at Newport News Shipyard, a three-master (*Sallie L'on*), four-master (*Malcolm Baxter*), five-master (*Jennie French*), and six-master (*Eleanor A. Perry*).

were built through the 1800's, especially in Maine, to power larger hulls and carry heavier loads.

Three-masted schooners first appeared around 1800, and during the 1830's were built in growing numbers in Maine at Ellsworth, Eden, Bristol, and Blue Hill. The three-masters, or "terns," were also "a favorite rig of Canada's Maritime Provinces."

The first four-master was built at Bath in 1880, although some other hulls had been converted to four masts earlier—for example, the *Victoria* in San Francisco in 1864, and the *Wey-bosset* on the East Coast in 1879. Four-masters proliferated, with hundreds built on both American coasts. In about 1900, these were used up and down the coasts of Canada, the United States, the West Indies, and South America, with some trans-

Atlantic crossings to Europe and West Africa. Over the years up to World War I, between 700 and 800 big schooners were built and operated by Nova Scotians alone. It is estimated that approximately 130 four-masted schooners were built on the East Coast during just the four years 1917 to 1920.

Hand hoisting of sails gave way to steam-powered and then gasoline-powered hoisting or "donkey" engines, introduced to save "work, wages and food." And, without the need for boilers and fuel storage space that the steamships required, the large schooners had that much more payload capacity. A big, four-master could carry 500 to 700 tons and be crewed by as few as eight sailors.

The first five-masted schooner—the *Governor Ames*—was built at Waldoboro, Maine, in 1888. More than 140 of them were built on both coasts over the next 30 years before 1920. The French Government alone ordered 40, all with auxiliary steam machinery, to be built in Oregon and Washington.

The first six-master, the *George W. Wells*, was built at Camden, Maine, and launched in August 1900. In the first decade of the 20th century, Maine shipyards built all nine of the wooden six-masted schooners. (Nine additional six-masters were created between 1908 and 1943 by re-rigging steamers and four-masted barks.) Because of their sail configuration and great length, the six-masters were very fast, but most were also unwieldy. Their length-to-beam ratio of 6 ½ to 1, combined with large, unsupported booms and gaffs tended to make them difficult and dangerous to handle, especially compared to square-riggers.

Seven of the ten six-masted schooners were built by the Percy & Small yard at Bath

The larger, heavier loads also became unsupportable for the wooden hulls. Despite using huge "keelsons" of 15-inch-square timber and "sister keelsons" on either side, "hogging"—or bulging of the wooden hulls—was inevitable. This inspired the building of the steel-hulled six-master, the *William L. Douglas*, at Quincy, Massachusetts, in 1903. Seven of the ten six-masters (nine wooden and the single steel hull) were built at the yard of Percy & Small in Bath, Maine. That yard built a total of 41 four-to-six masters.

In an incredible coincidence, the first two six-masters—the *George W. Wells* and the *Eleanor A. Percy*, and the *only* two at the time—collided off Cape Cod in June of 1901, but neither sank then. All nine of the wooden six-masters were eventually lost at sea, seven as a result of Atlantic storms, and two from fire. Their average life was only 14 years.

The seven-masted schooner *Thomas W. Lawson* with its light-colored, relatively un-rusted hull, possibly on its inauguration day, July 10, 1902.

The captain's stateroom on the *Lawson*

One historian concluded that "The wooden six-masters built in Maine were maximum in size that was practical in the schooner." Nevertheless, in 1901, an eight-masted steel schooner was proposed, with a length of 400 feet, a beam of 52 feet, and a 30-foot draft, but it was never built. On June 25 of that year, however, a contract was signed to build a steel seven-master of approximately the same size.

THE *LAWSON*

THAT SCHOONER, the *Thomas W. Lawson*, was built the next year and was the final and most dramatic example of this last gasp in trying to make sail pay—and compete with steamships—with more cargo and smaller crews.

She was intended to show that sailing ships with small

crews could be more practical and economical than dirty coal-guzzling steamships.

The *Lawson* was built originally with an eye to sailing the Pacific Ocean, but spent her life primarily carrying coal between port cities on the Eastern Seaboard, especially between Norfolk, Virginia, and various New England ports, but also including ports as far away as the Gulf coast of Texas.

The *Lawson* was designed by Bowdoin B. Crowninshield, for the Coastwise Transportation Company of Boston. Crowninshield was a prolific naval architect from Marblehead, Massachusetts, and best known for his America's-class racing yachts. He designed some 1,500 vessels, and it has been said that, "any vessel built during his designing career qualifies to be on the National Register of Historic Vessels."

The schooner was built of steel and designated Hull Number 110 at the Quincy Yard of the Fore River Ship & Engine Building Company. From humble beginnings in 1884, this shipyard became the second largest in the United States, and was a leading shipbuilder for a century. Until late in the 20th century, Fore River built hundreds of vessels, ranging from schooners, to aircraft carriers and other navy vessels, to Liquefied Natural Gas (LNG) tankers.

The *Lawson* was launched on July 10, 1902, and delivered for service on September 10, 1902. Captain Arthur L. Crowley was her first master. He was the brother of the Coastwise president, John G. Crowley, and had supervised the building of the *Lawson*. Before the *Lawson*, Arthur Crowley had been master of the first six-master *George W. Wells*. The *Lawson*'s total cost was estimated to be less than $300,000. (Later, John Crowley said $280,000.)

The *Lawson* "represented the ultimate overstretching of the schooner principle." The vessel was 404 feet long, with a 50-foot beam and a 35-foot vertical dimension. When she was fully loaded, the schooner is said to have drawn 32 feet. With a steel hull, she would not be plagued with the problem of "hogging," common to the large wooden schooner hulls. The *Lawson* weighed 5,218 tons, with a deadweight cargo capacity of approximately 8,000 tons—more for coal, some said—and an overall displacement of well over 10,000 tons. At age five in 1907, her tonnage and deadweight capacity still was the largest of any American-owned ocean-going vessel.

She had two steel decks, a tier of widely-spaced hold beams, a poop forward of the aftermast, and a windless under the top-gallant forecastle. She had six cargo hatches, holds 35 feet deep, and was fitted with anti-rolling bilge keels.

She required only 16 men with only 12 deckhands, owing to the use of small steam donkey engines to handle the sails, anchors, cargo, steering, and pumping. There was a donkey engine at the foot of each mast, to raise and lower the sails, plus another for the anchors, each of which weighed 10,000 pounds. Two verti-cal boilers—one forward and one aft—powered it all, including providing heat, electric lights and telephone communications throughout the vessel. A steamship of comparable size would have required a crew of 35 to 50, and even a conventional sail-ing vessel would have needed 28—compared to the 16 men for the *Lawson*.

Thomas W. Lawson, the man, still prominent in 1918, but his wealth-forming years were behind him, 11 years after his schooner's demise.

Because the steam engines were not fitted—and could not be used—for propulsion, the *Lawson* was a true sailing vessel, the largest ever.

The schooner was named for Thomas W. Lawson, a prominent Boston stockbroker and speculator, yachtsman, and author. By 1900, the businessman Lawson was worth at least $50 million (the equivalent of $1.5 billion today), and he built a huge and famous house, called *Dreamwold*, in Scituate, near Boston, at a cost of some $6 million. The same year as the ship's launch, Lawson co-published a book *The Lawson History of the America's Cup*, the race for which he had recently built his own yacht entry.

Lawson—the man—was famous as the "Copper King," as a result of helping the Standard Oil Company make a killing on the restructuring of Amalgamated Copper mines and properties. He

At age five in 1907, the *Lawson*'s tonnage and deadweight capacity still was the largest of any American-owned ocean-going vessel.

had a stormy relationship with the Standard Oil interests, and after 1902 became a well-published, well-known and caustic critic of big business and the "money kings."

Lawson had a significant ownership in Coastwise, and the seven-master was named in his honor. He often referred to the *Lawson* as "the grandest seabird which ever floated."

THE EYE OF THE BEHOLDER

MARITIME HISTORIAN Basil Lubbock described the *Lawson*'s hull as having "the lines of a canal bridge and looking about as sweet as a bathtub." The hull was originally painted light steel gray and white and "from a distance looked a bit like a picket fence." But, within two years, the hull was changed to black. Some later photographs show streaks of rust running down the massive iron sides, but thanks to the black-and-white photography of the time, these pictures do not make the *Lawson* look as ugly as she might have appeared from time to time in person. Said one critical observer, "... no unbiased eye could see her as beautiful."

With her sails unfurled and at sea, however, the vessel's appearance was quite extraordinary. Captain Dow's niece recalls:

My mother and I watched her sail down Boston Harbor from our porch up on the hill in Quincy ... She was in full sail and was a magnificent sight that beautiful day.

And, a lifetime resident of Hooper Island in Chesapeake Bay also remembers her beauty and notoriety:

We saw the Lawson *once from here on the Island. As she sailed up the Bay word spread around the community of her presence, and many came out to look and admire this beautiful ship, and wonder in awe about what great things or marvels would be done yet by the hand of man. People stood on their steps or lined the shore to watch. The ship was a magnificent sight to behold ...*

THE MASTS

T HE LOWER MASTS were constructed of steel and were 135 feet tall, and Oregon pine topmasts added another 58 feet. Her foremost mast was 33 inches in diameter, and the other six were all 30 inches thick.

From the beginning, there was controversy about what each of the seven masts should be called, because there never before had been seven to name on a single vessel. Different names were advocated and used by designer Crowley, some members of the crew, and the world at large later in the *Lawson's* life.

The following sets of mast names have been used:

At Launch	After Launch	Captain Crowley	Some Crews	Eventual
Fore	Forecastle	Fore	Monday	One
Main	Fore	Main	Tuesday	Two
Mizzen	Main	Mizzen	Wednesday	Three
Spanker	Mizzen	Four	Thursday	Four
Jigger	Jigger	Five	Friday	Five
Driver	Spanker	Six	Saturday	Six
Pusher	After	Spanker	Sunday	Seven

The primary confusion surrounded what to call the fourth, fifth, and sixth masts, given that the first three and the last one were often agreed to be Fore, Main, Mizzen, and Spanker, respectively. In the end, using numbers for all seven became the norm.

THE SAILS

FULLY RIGGED, the *Lawson* carried 25 sails: seven gaffsails, seven topsails, six staysails, and five jibs. The sails used 43,055 square feet—or about an acre—of canvas, weighing 18 tons, and made by the firm of Dunn & Elliot, in Thomaston. The rigging alone for each mast weighed about three tons.

The *Lawson's* 69-foot long steel-spiked bowsprit was fitted with a martingale.

THE FIRST FIVE YEARS

IN THE YEARS following its launch in 1902, the *Lawson* plied the East Coast, delivering coal and other commodities between Boston and other cities down the coast to Texas. Coastwise Transportation remained the owner. The company's President remained John G. Crowley, brother of Arthur Crowley, the *Lawson's* first captain.

From the start, the *Lawson* proved unstable, especially when empty, and temperamental when partially loaded. Her length-to breadth ratio of eight-to-one was unstably high. Even Crown-inshield, her designer who had said she handled like a yacht, candidly wrote later: "Light she was all right with a leading wind, but tacking in moderate weather was sometimes difficult and occasionally impossible." She would sail best only when fully loaded, because this kept more of her hull under water and out of the wind—that is, less freeboard. But, her draft then exceeded the depths of most harbors destined to receive the cargo. A sailor once commented that the *Lawson* handled "like a beached whale." And, "the story goes that it took half an hour to bring her about."

At one point, while docked at the Port of New Orleans, the *Lawson* blew over and had to be up-righted.

The *Lawson* was designed to haul coal and other dry cargoes. But, in 1906, she was converted into an oil tanker and leased to the Sun Oil Company of Philadelphia, to carry oil from Sun's terminal at Sabine Pass, Port Arthur, Texas, to their refinery at Marcus Hook, Pennsylvania. Rates for coal had fallen below 60 cents per hundredweight, making coal an uneconomic cargo. They converted the hold into 14 tanks. While she was being rebuilt at the Newport News Shipbuilding & Drydock Company, water leaked through her wooden bulkheads, the weight shifted, and she started to roll over. But, her spring lines held until the imbalance could be corrected. Another potential foundering while in port had been averted.

Edward Rowe relates a story of the schooner capsizing at Sabine Pass. She had rolled over on her port beam ends, completely blocking 10 steamers and other commercial ships from passing in either direction. Arthur Crowley, of Coastwise, ordered Rowe to help, and the engineer climbed aboard the hull and concluded that someone had probably left a series of giant valves on the starboard side closed during the loading. He waded across the submerged deck, found the six 24-inch valve wheels, and opened each of them. Over the net two hours the *Lawson*'s masts came up as she righted herself.

The capsizing had sprung and ruined the 12-inch square wooden bulkheads, but it was decided to load her up and sail to Philadelphia anyway. Rowe was appointed chief engineer on the *Lawson*. The tug *Paul Jones* began towing the schooner north and encountered a virtual hurricane off Cape Canaveral Florida. With the tow line cut, the *Paul Jones* staggered into the Charleston, South Carolina, harbor badly battered. The *Lawson* successfully broke out its storm sails and made Delaware Breakwater. And, another tug towed her to Chester, Pennsylvania, near Philadelphia, where the crew discharged her cargo at the Sun Oil refinery there at Marcus Hook.

After a complete refitting—including the replacement of the wooden bulkheads with steel ones at the dry dock in Brooklyn, New York—the *Lawson* was again ready for sea duty and was towed back to Philadelphia.

Although ideal for the wind and wave conditions near shore, schooners in general did not fare well in the open sea where their relatively short masts could, in the trough of a storm-driven wave, fall below the wind and then be "slammed mercilessly while on the crest." The sails of the taller, square-rigged clipper ships could remain firmly in the wind at all times, and could keep a more steady pace across the waves.

In 1907, the *Lawson* was chartered to use its vast hull to

deliver bulk oil from East Coast refineries to markets across the Atlantic in Europe, where demand for diesel, heating and lubricating oil, and gasoline, was growing rapidly. This would be the first transatlantic voyage of her career.

SAILING TO ENGLAND

I N NOVEMBER of 1907, Sun Oil set plans for the *Lawson* to carry a little more than two million gallons of oil from Philadelphia to Germany, by way of London. The cargo—which has been referred to as gasoline, fuel oil, paraffin oil, lubricating oil, kerosene, and other distillates—was worth about $200,000 at the time. The trip was to be the *Lawson*'s first trans-Atlantic voyage, with her new captain, George W. Dow.

THE CAPTAIN

C APTAIN DOW, "from a well-known seafaring family in Hancock," had been asked to take command of the *Lawson* because of his long record of sailing the world's oceans, on both schooners and square riggers, as well as his long and successful association with the John S. Emery Company. He also was then considered by seafarers to be one of the "lucky captains," because he had been at sea for 40 years and was still alive.

Later, the *Lawson*'s engineer commented "Captain Dow, an old square-rigger master, wouldn't take any advice from schooner men, although he was sailing the world's largest schooner ... " Although it is true that he had more years of square-rigging experience, Captain Dow had also spent more than 10 years in command of schooners.

Approached by Arthur or John Crowley of the *Lawson*'s owner Coastwise Transportation, Captain Dow was engaged as the *Lawson*'s new master in the late summer of 1907, taking over from her previous captains Arthur Crowley, Emmons Babbitt, and Elliot Gardner. He oversaw the schooner's steel bulkhead refitting in Brooklyn during the late summer and early fall. On September 4, 1907, Captain Dow's son Richard received a postcard in Melrose from his friend, Ed, in New York:

> *Dick.*
> *Was over to see your father yesterday. He took us all over the ship. Am taking a few pictures. Don't know how good they will be until I get home. Will be home Fri night.*
>
> —Ed

On Friday, October 12, 1907, the *Lawson* sailed up New York Harbor, on what would be her last visit to the City. The Cunard liner *Lusitania* was there too, and both reached the Quarantine Station at about the same time. What a coincidence to have the world's largest steamship and largest sailing vessel arrive together.

The Captain arrived in Philadelphia for the voyage to Europe at the beginning of November. His wife was at home in Melrose, and his two grown sons lived and worked in Boston.

THE CREW

WHEN CAPTAIN DOW received his new command, he sought out and recruited 34-year old Bent Libby as his Chief Mate, even though Libby had left seafaring, was married, and had a good position with Armour & Co. in Boston. Libby had risen to be Mate on the *Auburndale* with Dow, and was somewhat in the Captain's debt. Although he was reluctant to go, he agreed solely because he felt he owed Dow. That act of gratitude was to cost him his life. He signed on for $80 per month, with his wife Annie and their family of five children to wait patiently for his return to their home in Marlboro, Massachusetts.

Libby and the second mate, named Crocker, reported to Captain Dow aboard the *Lawson* on November 4, 1907. During the next ten days, the schooner loaded her cargo of just over two million gallons, and brought on the remainder of her crew of 18 men with a broad mix of nationalities. On November 15, the captain went to the Old Custom House on Chestnut Street and changed the *Lawson* from a Permanent to a Temporary registration, in order to proceed with foreign trade. He listed the owners as: Coastwise Transp. Co. 61/64; C.H. Delano, Taunton 1/128; Emily W.R. Bullard, New Bedford 1/128; Geo. A. VonLingen, Baltimore 1/64; and Arthur Orr, Chicago 1/64.

While Captain Dow was completing the paperwork away from the schooner, six of the seamen became dissatisfied with their pay or something else and quit the ship. The six were the Wiklund brothers from Sweden, Burgess from Maine, O'Brien of Dublin, Edwards of Barbados, and Smith from Yarmouth. Six replacements were quickly signed after the paperwork was completed and the *Lawson* cleared to leave. "It was a true pier head jump—but it was a jump straight to their deaths." It was a motley crew that made ready to sail, comprising nine nationalities, with an average age of 28 ½ years (26 ½ excluding the captain), and pay averaging $30 per month.

As recorded by the United States shipping commissioner at Philadelphia, the crew was:

Position	Name	Hometown	Age
Captain	George W. Dow	Melrose, MA	61
First Mate	Bent P. Libby	Marlboro, MA	34 †
Second Mate	O. Crocker	New York, NY	40 †
Steward	George Miller	Boston, MA	37 †
Cabin Boy	Mark Sanson	Brooklyn, NY	17 †
Engineer	Edward Longfellow Rowe	Wiscasset, ME	34
Firemen	John Krase	Sweden	38 †
	Z. Olanssen	Sweden	36 †
Seamen	Gust England	Norway	28 †
	John Lunde	Norway	25 †
	Ole Olsen	Denmark	21 †
	P.A. Burke	Tonawanda, NY	25 †
	L. Garridon	Caracas, Venezuela	22 †
	N. Petersen	Riga, Latvia/Russia	24 †
	George W. Allen	London, England	27 †
	A. Peterson	Denmark	26 †
	Gustav Bohnke	Berlin, Germany	27 †
	Anton Andrade	Austria	24 †

Although the schooner had no engine or propeller, an engineer was nevertheless required to keep up and run a diesel oil generator to drive the electric winches to hoist the sails on all seven masts. Edward Rowe had a year earlier been taken on as the *Lawson*'s engineer, and Captain Dow inherited him with the schooner.

With the confusion of replacing a third of the crew just prior to sailing, the exact number and identity of crewmembers—and, as a result, the number of crew eventually lost—remain uncertain. There were reputedly two unnamed and last-minute crewmembers who may have been aboard, and some accounts show a crew of 19 or 20. But, there is no clear evidence that more than 18 sailed.

Another seaman, Niels Anton Nielsen from Denmark, signed on the *Lawson* but for some reason missed the sailing in Philadelphia. After subsequently circumnavigating the globe seven times as a navy and merchant marine sailor, he retired to raise chickens in New Hampshire.

THE CROSSING

EMBARKING on its 3,800-mile trip to London, the *Lawson* sailed from the Marcus Hook refinery and oil terminal on the Delaware River near Philadelphia on November 19, 1907, assisted by the tug *Paraguay*. Sailing off toward the open water of the Atlantic 100 miles away, the giant schooner grounded briefly in the river and required up to a dozen tugs to help float her off to be on her way. Passing the Delaware Breakwater to starboard and Cape May Point to port, she fixed her course for the winter seas of the North Atlantic.

"Nineteen-hundred-seven was one of those years when there was plenty of wind." Severe storms plagued the scheduled departure and the entire trip. Just beyond the Delaware Breakwater, the wind came around northwest and they "ran with a free sheet." As the wind blew stronger and stronger,

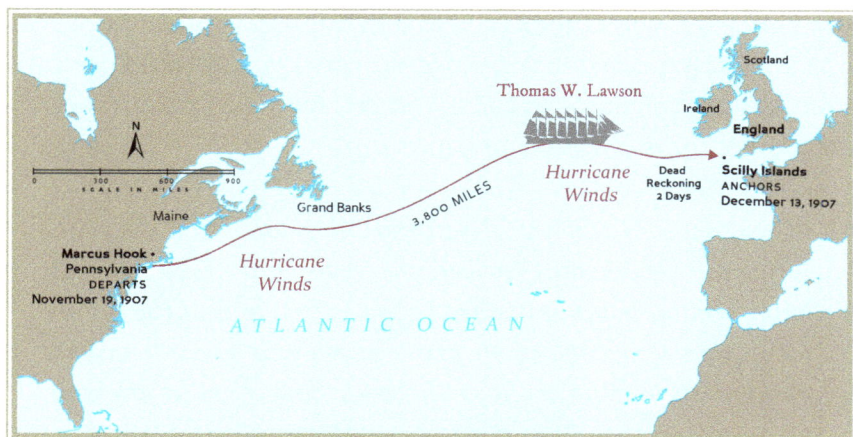

Plagued by storms, the Lawson takes 24 days to arrive in English waters on Friday, December, 13, 1907.

they took in the spanker and topsails, but by the time they passed the Grand Banks of Newfoundland, the *Lawson* had lost all her main sails. Engineer Rowe estimated the wind at 80 knots, and the schooner's speed at 14 to 16 knots. They sped past many steamers. After three days, with the wind having reached an estimated 100 miles an hour at some points (according to Rowe), they had outrun the hurricane, and the crew hoisted the triangular storm sails.

Well past the Grand Banks, the second severe episode began on Monday, December 9—the *Lawson*'s 20th day at sea—with a southerly gale lasting all day and continuing straight through Tuesday and Wednesday. In nearly a month of on-and-off strong gales, she was "washed from end to end." Most of the canvas was torn away, all her lifeboats were smashed, and her rafts washed overboard. Deck fittings were smashed, including hatches and the cabin door. She had only six usable sails and a 20-foot boat left on board.

On Thursday, December 12, she was approaching the English Channel in fog. Unable to take observations, Captain Dow had been on dead reckoning for two days, with no certain idea of their position. Recalled the captain:

> *It was late Thursday afternoon when we first encountered the storm that proved the vessel's undoing. For a time, we made good headway against it, but as the wind increased and the storm grew in fury, it soon became evident that the ship was in great danger. She pitched violently and, despite the heroic efforts of the men, she got beyond our control. Giant waves washed over the deck, and the ship rocked from side to side, so that it was almost impossible to keep on our feet on the deck.*

The next day—Friday, the 13th of December—the *Lawson* approached the British Isles from the west. The Captain's plans were to make landfall 10 miles south of Bishop Rock. Unbeknownst to them, a giant low-pressure system was sweeping in on Europe from the west, reaching from Ireland to the north and France to the south..

SCILLY

THE ISLES OF SCILLY comprise 56 islands—basically large, white granite rocks, rising above the sea's surface here and there over an area of about 80 square miles. They lie 29 miles west of Land's End, the English mainland's westernmost tip.

The islands are the exposed tops of hills that have been slowly submerged since prehistoric times by a rising sea. Separation of Scilly from the mainland took place some 10,000 years ago, following the last ice age, but separation of the islands from each other within Scilly occurred much more recently—from about 700 A.D.—and is continuing. The water depth among many of the islands is only 45 feet or less. During the lowest tides, it is possible to walk on the sandbars among the islands of Tresco, Bryher and Samson, and a good distance out from St. Martin's toward both Tresco and St. Mary's.

Inhabitants of Scilly date from the Bronze Age, and Christian hermits lived on some of the islands since about 400 A.D. Kings took refuge here, and the Duchy of Cornwall has owned the islands from 1337. From Scilly, Pirates plundered passing ships in the mid 1600's.

The islands are small and low, totaling a mere 10 square miles in area, with the highest point rising to only 165 feet above mean sea level. Many of the islands are within a mile of two or three others, giving the impression to a person standing on a shore, that the other land is literally a stone's throw away. Small ferryboats, or launches, carry passengers—and anything else—from island to island. They have been piloted by members of the Hicks family for at least 150 years, and some still are.

INHABITED ISLANDS

ONLY FIVE ISLANDS are inhabited. St. Mary's, the main island, has about 1,700 residents, and the populations fall off fast from there, with about 180 people on Tresco, 140 on St.

Martin's, 92 on Bryher, and 73 on St. Agnes. The population of Scilly overall has declined during the last two centuries—from more than 2,600 in 1822, to about 2,200 today. Although the population of St. Mary's grew nearly 15%, the population of all the others has fallen by nearly two-thirds.

St. Mary's, the largest of the islands, is only 2 ½ miles across at its widest and covers about 1,550 acres. It is the center of island life and all commerce and transportation. It has an airport, the only golf course, remains of an old Garrison built in 1742, the Old Town Church with a graveyard heavily populated with wreck victims, the excellent Scilly museum, and an active Quay. Hughtown is the only true town on the islands, with about two dozen shops. As on all the inhabited islands, there are excellent sandy beaches around St. Mary's.

Tresco is the next largest island, less than a mile to the northwest of St. Mary's, and, with 730 acres, is only half as large. A Benedictine priory was located here by the 12th century. The 20 acres of sub-tropical gardens at Tresco Abbey contain more than 5,000 species from 100 countries, including banana, cinnamon and citrus trees. Augustus Smith began the gardens in 1834. King Charles' Castle—high on the northern-most hill and built in 1550—and its nearby replacement, Cromwell's Castle from 1661—were built to defend the islands against attack by the Dutch. The island of Bryher adjoins Tresco to the west, across a channel only a few hundred yards wide that separates the two rock islands.

St. Martin's is about two miles to the northeast of St. Mary's, totals about 585 acres, and has some of the islands' finest beaches. The Seven Stones rocks lie seven miles east of St. Martin's, about a quarter of the distance to the English mainland.

St. Agnes seems more remote than the one mile of water separating it from St. Mary's. St. Agnes is the inhabited island farthest west in Scilly—toward the scattered, treacherous Western Rocks and the primary shipping lanes—and overlooks barren Annet Island and Hellweathers, less than a mile farther west. St. Agnes, including its uninhabited adjacent part Gugh, measures less than a mile square and 360 acres. St. Agnes has only about 70 residents and no hotels. In 1878, the heads of 17 of the 25 households living there had the surname Hicks, and this family has lived on St. Agnes for nearly four centuries.

St. Agnes is also home to the Scilly's first lighthouse, which was completed in 1680 and served continuously until 1911. It is kept whitewashed and serves as an important day mark for Scilly sailors.

St. Agnes had its own lifeboat until 1920, when the service was consolidated with the other Royal National Lifeboat Institution (R.N.L.I.) boat on St. Mary's. In 1907, the longest lifeboat slip in Britain was on St. Agnes at Periglis.

POSITION AND CLIMATE

CITIZENS OF SCILLY—called Scillonians—have been a proud, self-sufficient and largely independent people for centuries. As one Scillonian says, "The Cornish don't think of themselves as English, and in turn we don't think of ourselves as English or Cornish." Transportation to the mainland has never been easy. A daily (except Sunday) boat between Penzance and St. Mary's takes two hours 45 minutes, and is often a rough passage. Helicopter service was introduced in 1964 and cuts the trip to 20 minutes, and there are regular flights available on small planes from several Cornwall airports. Scheduled air service was not introduced until 1937, when biplanes used the fifth fairway on the St. Mary's golf course as a landing strip.

The Gulf Stream passes across the Atlantic from the Caribbean to just west of the Scilly's and provides the islands with a mild climate. The name Scilly is derived from an ancient word for sun or sunny. Air temperatures vary from highs of 66 Fahrenheit in July and August, to 48 in January and February. Lows are not much lower, at 57 in August, and 43 in January and February. Frosts and snow are rare. "It may therefore be claimed that Scilly is as warm in winter as the French Riviera, and that winter nights in Scilly are as warm as spring nights in London." Flowers for export to the mainland in the spring remain an important industry, and scores of migrant birds invade the islands to nest in the spring and fall.

The seas around Scilly are blue and clear, with visibility to the bottom often 20 feet or more in still water. The air also is exceedingly clear and free of haze or pollution.

Although the temperature is relatively mild, exposure to the full force of ocean currents and the prevailing west winds frequently combine to form fierce running seas moving from west to east. Three-story-high waves are common. Tides vary from eight to 16 feet, depending on the phases of the moon. And, the Rennel Current also occasionally pushes northward from south of the islands at the mouth of the English Channel.

TREACHERY FOR SHIPS

THE ROCKS AND ISLANDS of the Western Rocks—known to sailors of old as "the Dogs of Scilly"—have been the graveyard of many ships. The islands and the huge rock ledges and reefs just below the water's surface, combined with the strong prevailing winds and currents, leave ships at sea little room for error in safely navigating to or through Scilly. Over the centuries, shipwrecks have been central to Scilly's identity, as the islands stand at the entrance to one of the world's busiest shipping channels. Most estimates place the number of vessels wrecked in the islands at between 800 and 900, over the last 400 years. The power of bringing in ships was also attributed to St. Warna, an Irish saint, who, according to legend, landed at the cove of the same name, on St. Agnes. "If these rocks could cry," one of St. Mary's bus drivers said, "the sea level would rise."

As inevitable and unfortunate as they may be, shipwrecks have, over the centuries, provided Scillonians with windfalls of salvaged goods. Perhaps this led to a reluctance to build a lighthouse in the islands until 1680. And, when the St. Agnes light was coal-fired, it was alleged that fuel was deliberately neglected, "in order to mislead ships and attract lucrative wrecks."

This conflict between the tragedy of shipwrecks and the

Referred to as "The Dogs of Scilly," these rocks,
just west of Annet, include Shag Rock

accompanying local material benefits is rationalized in a 1780
prayer by Reverend John Troutbeck:

We pray, O Lord, not that wrecks should happen,
But that, should they happen,
Thou wilt guide them into these islands
For the benefit of the poor inhabitants.

And, happily:

Stories of cows left to wonder on the coast with lights
attached to their tails to confuse ships at sea have never
been substantiated.

The current lighthouse, situated on a tiny island called Bishop's Rock, marks the western edge of the islands, six miles west
of St. Mary's. The lighthouse was begun in 1847, because the

St. Agnes lighthouse—being five miles to the east—was too far away for ships to see in time to avoid the perilous Western Rocks, especially during fog or storms. In February 1850, after three years work, the cast-iron tower was destroyed without a trace by a fierce storm before it was completed. Beginning in 1852, another attempt was made, using blocks of Cornish granite. The light finally went on in 1858, but powerful vibrations and cracks soon began to develop. At one point, waves more than 130 feet high broke over the lighthouse, washing away the light and pouring water into the tower. Beginning in 1881, 3,000 more tons of stone were added around the existing tower, and some 55 feet in height was added. This has provided the height and strength needed to survive the storms since the 1880's. With a height of 143 feet, *The Bishop* is the tallest lighthouse in Britain. On a clear night, its light can be seen from 24 miles out.

St. Agnes Lighthouse, established in 1680 and one of the oldest in the United Kingdom, looks over Smith Sound, the island of Annet, and treacherous rocks just beyond.

A ship heading from the Americas east toward northern Europe will encounter The Bishop as the first landfall after crossing the North Atlantic. "The best approach tactic is to keep well clear of the area." If the ship passes safely to the south—or right—of The Bishop, it can move, unobstructed, into the English Channel and toward the main ports of southern

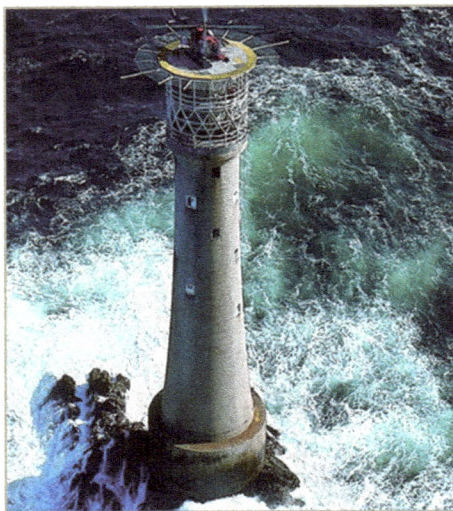

The Bishop Rock Lighthouse as it stands today,
with service helicopter on deck

England and Continental Europe. "Aim to leave Bishop Rock light about three miles clear to the North ..." If, on the other hand, the ship passes to the north—or left—of the Bishop, it will pass directly into the Isles of Scilly. "The leading marks are distant and good visibility is required. There are no suitable anchorages. Tidal streams are strong ..."

LANDFALL

THE APPROACH

AS THE *LAWSON* approached the British Isles from the west in raging seas with little visibility, it was critical that the ship pass well to the South of the Bishop, as planned. About mid-day, the Captain and crew saw the light of what they thought was a passing ship to the leeward (south), but were actually seeing the Bishop Rock light. As a result, the *Lawson* passed the lighthouse on the North side—and sailed directly into the Scilly's.

At about 1:00 p.m. on Friday the 13th, the winds and seas were increasing and Captain Dow found himself too close in to sail on ahead through the islands, and with too little sail to reverse his course and tack back around the Bishop. The danger was exacerbated by the running easterly tide. He decided to bring the *Lawson* to, drop anchor and wait. In his words:

> *Finally, when we were almost abreast the Scilly Islands, I decided that it was useless to make any further attempt against such odds, and we sought out an anchorage that would be safe at least for a time. Then, we sent out signals of distress.*

WAITING OUT THE NIGHT

WHEN THE AIR CLEARED slightly later in the afternoon, the men on the *Lawson* found themselves trapped inside the crim—the dangerous arc of the Western Rocks. Unable to alter course there in Broad Sound, they hoped to wait out the storm and then go back the correct way. They were anchored between the rocks Gunners and Nundeeps, with Annet Island directly in their path. A high cliff on Annet, called Annet Head, was visible only a short distance away.

Engineer Rowe relates: "I looked down over the port bow and could easily see the breakers. I know we were approaching trouble, and jumped up and let go the port bower." The *Lawson* began to swing and cleared the Hellweather Reef by only a few feet. Captain Dow ordered the starboard anchor let go too. It was after 4:00 p.m. and getting dark. They now had 900 feet of chain out with the port anchor, and 540 feet with the starboard anchor.

The Bishop Lighthouse fired a distress flare to call out the St. Agnes lifeboat. The wind then was west-southwest blowing "about seven or eight," or between 35 and 50 miles per hour, with a drizzly rain. Thirteen men assembled at the lifeboat station and slips in Periglis on St. Agnes and set out in the lifeboat *Charles Deere James*. The ten oarsmen—five on each side—included William Thomas Hicks (known as Billy Cook), his son Frederick Charles Hicks (known to all as Freddie Cook), Obadiah Hicks, William Francis Hicks, James Thomas Hicks, William Trenary, Albert Hicks, Stephen Lewis Hicks, Frederick Osbert Hicks (Fred), his brother John Horace Hicks (Jack) and Walter Long (a "coastguard" from St. Mary's). In addition, there were two coxswains—William George Mortimer and Abraham James Hicks, the father of James Thomas. (Some sources cite a James Hicks and Benjamin Hicks instead of Albert Hicks and Walter Long. However, James and Benjamin have not been corroborated.)

Because only sails and oars powered the lifeboat, they had to row about 20 minutes out from Periglis far enough to set the sail safely. They made sail toward Annet Head. The wind was not then blowing hard, but the seas were rough. Because they were aiming west into the wind, they had to go just to the windward of Annet and then back northward again, and then southward again, beating like that all the way, until they got towards Gunners and the *Lawson* came into sight.

She was about a mile and a half from Annet Head, at anchor, and was not riding heavily in the waves, because of her extreme length. The wind was freshening all the time, and the coxswain said: "Lash yourselves in, every one of you, because I am easing for nothing." The boat would fill up with water each time it broke through a wave, but would more or less empty herself out by the open safety valves. They continued on and on beating their way, eventually reaching the huge ship, sometime between 5:00 and 6:00 p.m.. The *Charles Deere James* went straight to the windward (north) side of the *Lawson*, and the crew pulled down the two sails and rowed alongside.

As John Horace Hicks describes: "She was like a forest, all the masts one behind the other. It was from here to next week the length of her—enormous she was."

By then it was dark—in mid-December—and the water very rough. Captain Dow came to the side and said to the lifeboat crew, "Hallo."

"Do you realize where you are, Captain?", said coxswain Mortimer.

"Yes, I am in the Scilly Isles."

"Yes, but do you realize the dangerous position you are in?"

"Oh, I'm all right."

"Well, you are not all right."

"I've got both my anchors down and I've ridden out worse storms than this on the American side. I've had boats on either side of me drag their anchors and go aground but mine have held—I'm all right."

"Beg your pardon, but you are not all right. You may have ridden out storms on the other side of the Atlantic Ocean, but not where you are now."

They asked the Captain to abandon ship, but he refused. He asked, "Have you a Trinity House pilot aboard?"

"Yes", they informed him.

"Will he come aboard?"

It was customary for the pilots to take turns in guiding and assisting ships in predicaments, and it was Abraham James Hicks' turn (the lifeboat's second coxswain).

So, he was asked, "Abraham James, are you going aboard?"

"No, I am not", he responded.

"Why not?" they asked.

"We are here on lifesaving service and I am not leaving this boat."

"All right, if you're not going, I will", said Billy Cook Hicks.

"Put the ladder over the side."

They drew alongside the massive, iron hull. Because the wind and waves were stronger than ever in the dark—the wind had risen to an estimated "ten now easily"—they feared the small boat would be smashed against the side. So, they dropped around the stern, below the large warp, and waited for Billy Cook to talk to the Captain aboard the ship, where they remained from about 5:30 until 9:00 p.m.. After a while, Billy Cook called out over the stern, "Are you all right? I am sending you a can or a couple of cans of hot drink and some biscuits.

You can't get alongside no more. I'm remaining here all night, so make yourselves comfortable for the night."

Meanwhile, at about 4:25 p.m., a boat from the island of St. Mary's—the *Henry Dundas*—had also been dispatched. Upon reaching the ship at about 5:00 p.m. and attempting to get alongside in the rolling sea, her mainmast had snapped against the *Lawson's* hull below the quarterdeck. After about an hour, the crippled *Henry Dundas* returned to St. Mary's for repairs and also to telegram for tugs from Falmouth, at the request of Captain Dow. Later, the reply came that tugs had been dispatched at 10:20 that night, but had turned back, as the gale was too fierce.

The Captain recalled later:

> *The lifesavers answered and the brave men who man the lifeboats that came to us, did their best to reach the schooner and take us off, but the odds were against them. One of them lost her masts and was wallowing about in the sea herself almost helpless, but not once did the men waver.*

> *Time and again they attempted to get near enough to take our men off, but the Lawson was rocking so violently that it meant sure death to them, and so after a consultation with my men we sent them back, for we preferred to take our own chances against the storm, rather than to have those brave men go down.*

By seven or eight o'clock at night, the crew of the *Charles Deere James* had been in the water for nearly four hours. They wrapped themselves in the sails in the bottom of the boat, had their coffee and biscuits and made themselves as comfortable as they could in their 'oilers', life jackets and sails in the heaving sea. Soon, a tremendous wave broke over the boat, filling it to the gunwales. After the water had drained partially, the coxswain said, "Something has happened here, boys."

"What's the matter?"

"Don't know."

They tried to revive William Francis with brandy from a mug, but he was just like a dead man, having collapsed in the bottom of the boat.

"What are we going to do? We can't stay here like this. The man may die or be dead. Shout up to the pilot."

It was blowing hard now, about 60 to 70 miles per hour. The pilot went to the stern, and they told him that William Francis was lying unconscious and they could not revive him. They asked the pilot, "What about it?"

"You cannot get alongside—you'll smash your side in. The only thing to do is to take him ashore. That's the only answer."

"Will you come along with us? Come down over the warp and ask the Captain and crew to come as well, because if we go from you now to take this sick man ashore, it'll be impossible to get back again. It is blowing a hurricane now."

"Hold on a minute, I'll have a word with the Captain", the pilot yelled.

He soon came back shouting again:

"Alright. You go on ashore. I'm remaining here. The Captain guarantees his chains and anchors. Take William Francis ashore, but after you're ashore and get him right, keep an eye on me all night, for my riding lights, and if we get into trouble whatsoever, I'll fire rockets. Good night."

The lifeboat crew let go of the *Lawson*, raised their sail and ran home before the wind. The run was so powerful that the three-inch thick, five-foot long galvanized steel tiller was bent when they arrived at Periglis. They lit a green signal light to indicate they were coming. They carried William Francis to "Lewis's old place" and sent word to Dr. Brushfield on St. Mary's. The doctor "came over the Mr. Moyle," but William Francis did not regain consciousness until 8:30 the next morning. He evidently had had a heart attack when the huge wave broke on the boat. He had hastily jumped into the lifeboat without putting on oilskins, which no doubt had contributed to his exposure and suffering. Although he fully recovered, he never went in the lifeboat again.

This mission was the first service in a lifeboat for 17-year-old Jack Hicks. 50 years later, as the last living Trinity pilot, Jack Hicks observed, "It was the roughest night I have ever experienced at Scilly."

Jack Hicks (r) remembering the rescue in 1957.

The lifeboat crew changed into dry clothes in the St. Agnes lighthouse and kept close watch on the *Lawson*'s riding light. At about 2:50 in the morning, after a fierce squall, "the light went out and that was all." But, "it was not generally thought that a huge calamity had taken place." They had seen no rocket flare, so they were hopeful that the ship's lights had been temporarily extinguished by the squall. In total darkness, the islanders anxiously watched and waited.

MORNING

A T DAYBREAK on Saturday, with the air cleared somewhat, the group watching from the St. Agnes lighthouse saw only part of the hull—bottom up—and floating wreckage on the Outer Ranneys, as well as an oil slick on the water's surface all around St. Agnes and Annet. "The almost overwhelming stench of oil told its own story." The ship was a total wreck and had virtually disappeared.

As the storm had gotten worse and worse through the night, with the gale reaching an estimated 90 to 112 miles per hour, the waves and wind had strained the two anchor chains, plunging the ship over the huge waves, and pressuring her towards the jagged rocks nearby. From about 10:00 p.m., the schooner had begun to drag anchor. All those aboard were wearing lifejackets, except Captain Dow.

The port anchor chain came apart at about 1:15 in the morning, and the *Lawson* began to drag slowly on the starboard anchor. The Captain ordered distress signals be sent up, but the powder was "wet, soggy and worthless for firing." In any case, the weather would have made any lifeboat launch impossible had the flares worked and been seen.

The remaining starboard anchor chain snapped about an hour and a half later, at about 2:45 a.m., setting the ship adrift towards Annet. She swung around, heading for Hellweather's.

The next morning, only the *Lawson*'s capsized hull is visible, with stench of oil everywhere. Note the Bishop Rock Lighthouse about 3½ miles in the distance.

The Captain recalled: "When it became apparent that our ship was going on the rocks and nothing more could be done to save her, we distributed the life belts, and I ordered the men to the rigging."

The Captain and the Pilot climbed into the rigging of the seventh mast, or spanker, while the Engineer positioned himself near the shear pole. The other crewmembers were all forward near the bow. Each of them had about a fathom (six feet) of rope to lash themselves to the rigging, and the Engineer and the Captain passed the lashing around them and, without tying it tight, held the two ends in their hands. The Engineer thought the Pilot had made a hitch (that is, tied a knot) with his lashed rope.

Rowe, the Engineer, asked Pilot Hicks "if there was a chance of getting ashore. Hicks knew every inch of that treacherous part, and replied, 'No.'"

Almost at once the ship's starboard side struck rock broadside, west of Carn Irish. The rigging sagged, and the seven masts began to sway with the motion of the vessel, as she was buffeted by the huge seas and trembled from end to end. Quickly, she struck again, breaking in two between the sixth and seventh masts. The stern had been sliced right off; all masts and rigging crashed into the sea as well. In Dow's words:

> We had hardly gained good hold when the giant ship gave a lurch and in a minute more rolled over. Few of the men had a chance to unlash themselves from the rigging, and I really don't know how I got away myself.

To hear Engineer Rowe tell it:

> ... the Lawson struck on the jagged rocks ... All the crew, except the three of us, drowned at once ... After the Lawson had smashed her bow ashore, the great vessel started to swing to port, still pinioned on the ledge at her bow ... By then the Lawson had swung her side onto a sharp pinnacle apart ... As the stern of the Lawson came around to within sixty feet of a pinnacle, a giant wave hit against the top of the rock ledge. The backwash hit the shattered stern ... The great mast came battering down and I landed in the sea. The mast fell right on top of me, but somehow I retained consciousness.

A few feet away I could hear the pilot strangling to death in the rigging, but I couldn't help him. I had already untied my shoelaces, and now kicked my shoes off. You see, I never learned to swim. The ship fragments started to break up and the wooden bulkhead drifted alongside me. I grabbed hold of a projecting spike and was carried toward the rocky pinnacles ahead.

Still clinging to my spike, I watched as the stern drifted off by itself, the huge tank inside helping to keep it from sinking. It floated closer and closer to a giant outcropping of rocks, which had an ugly pinnacle.

A wave caught the stern, balanced it high on the crest, and smashed it against the rock, bursting the tank open like a ripe cantaloupe. Shivering momentarily, the stern slid into the sea and was gone. It is very deep water all around there.

I continued to drift along ... It was around daylight on Saturday the 14th that I struck bottom. Looking around me, I could see a reef extending toward the lighthouse. The tide was then ebbing, and I pushed my timber along toward the reef.

Soon I drifted close to a tall pinnacle, and grounded sixteen feet or so away from it. The water was awfully cold and had numbed me terribly, but I thought that there might be a way I could get across to the pinnacle and pull myself up before the tide started in again.

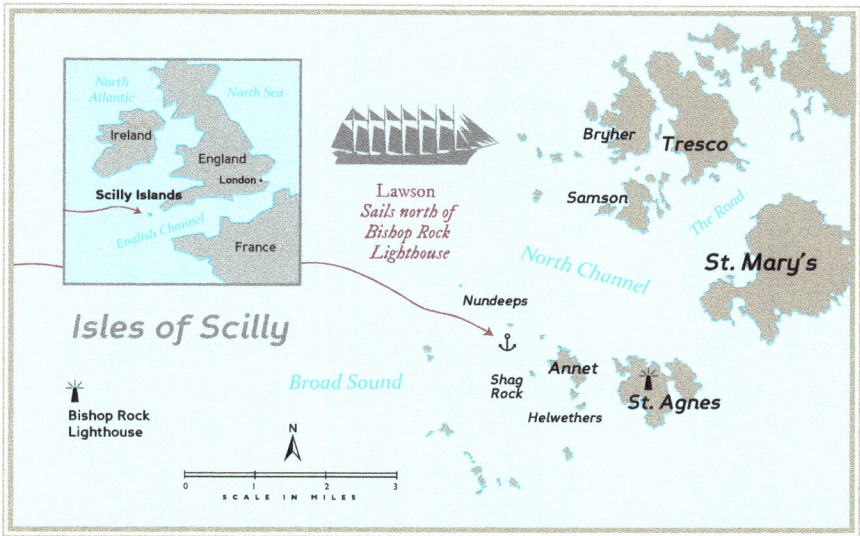

The *Lawson* mistakenly sails north of Bishop Rock lighthouse, finds herself in Broad Sound off Annet, and drops anchors on Friday afternoon.

Finally, I summoned all my strength, pushed away from the planking, and kicked with all my might. After a minute or so I found myself grounding on a mussel bed surrounded by white sand, and knew I wouldn't drown, at least for a while. It took some time to get my breath, but soon I started climbing to the top of the pinnacle, and got my hand in a crevice there. After I had a good rest I started to look around, hoping for rescue.

It was about two hours later that I noticed Captain Dow drifting toward me. He was encased in a life preserver, which he didn't have earlier. I clambered down toward the water, and when he drifted near enough I went over and pulled him above the current. He had a mackintosh around his arm.

The two men were too frozen to speak, as Rowe helped Dow to the pinnacle. It was obvious that the Captain was badly injured. In the crevice of the pinnacle, Rowe jammed his back against Dow's knees, to prevent the Captain from slipping, and Rowe's own knees were pressed against the rock being battered by the surf. Although Rowe did not know it, this pressure and battering had broken both his kneecaps.

The day after the wreck, the Captain remembered his struggle and meeting up with Rowe somewhat differently:

> *For two hours after the ship went over, I struggled in the sea and then was washed up on the rocks. Three times I clambered up on the rocks, only to be washed into the sea again, but finally I succeeded in hanging on, and then came another hour or more of perilous crawling over the rocks to a place of safety.*
>
> *During all this time I had not seen one of the men, but when shivering with cold and all but exhausted, I reached a sheltered place, there I found Engineer Rowe almost unconscious. Side by side we clung to the slippery rocks, holding each other on as the waves washed over us.*

The Captain had guaranteed his chains and anchors, with one chain out to its full 900-foot length and the other at 540 feet. Each chain link weighed 100 pounds. "One chain had parted like a bit of cotton, and when the second anchor struck the bottom, one of the flukes broke company." With most of the sails gone from the days of storms across the Atlantic, sailing away from the rocks was out of the question when the anchor cables tore loose.

The wind and waves had heaved the ship onto Shag Rock, just west of Annet and 1½ miles Northwest of St. Agnes. The impact had broken the ship in two, and the two halves quickly sank.

RESCUE

O N SATURDAY MORNING, when the group on St. Agnes saw that the ship had sunk, the wind was still blowing at hurricane force, and the seas were appallingly high and running. The weather was deemed still too rough to launch the lifeboat, despite the pleadings of Freddie Cook Hicks, who was terribly anxious about his father, the pilot left on the *Lawson*. Freddie Cook said, "Well, what about it—are we going to see if there is any life or anything at Annet?" He and seven others heroically volunteered to launch a 28-foot, six-oared gig, named the *Slippen*, to search for survivors on the rocks and ledges jutting out to the West and South of Annet Island.

Osbert Hicks, elected captain of the rescue effort and serving as the coxswain, was joined by Israel Hicks, Grenfell Legg, George

The Slippen and its crew the week after the Lawson rescue.

Mortimer, William Trenary, Fred Hicks, Freddie Cook Hicks, and Obadiah Hicks.

The last four had also gone out on the *Charles Deere James* the previous night. The others had been away on Friday, doing relief duty at the Round Island Lighthouse. When they were returning late Friday afternoon, they heard the signals fired by the Bishop Lighthouse and then saw the *Lawson* in Broad Sound. They made an attempt to reach her in their gig, but the weather was prohibitive, and they reached St. Agnes after the lifeboat had been launched.

Jack Hicks, Osbert's son, had gone out the night before, but his father forbade him to join the *Slippen* crew. Years later, while doing fieldwork side-by-side, Jack asked his father why he had not been allowed to go in the gig that morning. Osbert answered:

> There was only one reason. I never thought we should return. In that sea I never thought we had a chance, and I was in the boat and your brother. I thought you should stay behind and take over. That was my only reason.

The water remained treacherous on Saturday. At about 7:00 a.m., they all pulled the *Slippen* out from Periglis, a good distance to the water, as the tide was well down. Jack Hicks gave her a last push off, being the only one to be wearing high leather sea boots. None had yet donned lifejackets.

They soon spotted human forms on Annet Island but could not land for some time, due to the high seas. Eventually, about 8:00, they were able to land and found one dead body and wreckage strewn about, and then another three dead bodies lashed to wreckage. Then, they discovered George Allen—a seaman from Merrick Road in Battersea, London—sheltered behind a rock and faintly shouting for help. The soon-unconscious Allen was hauled aboard the *Slippen* and eventually stirred and was taken quickly back to St. Agnes, conscious but in great pain. He told them that he was returning to his aunt in London after five years at sea.

During a few minutes of consciousness, Allen said that even before the huge squall had hit, near 3:00 a.m., most of the deckhands had been washed overboard. The squall had thrown the *Lawson* onto her beam-ends, and she never recovered. The Captain, Mate and Pilot were last seen in the rigging. Allen had been out on the bowsprit and leaped onto the rock ledges when the schooner hit head on. He said that, at daybreak, he had seen life in the three others clinging to Annet, but the rescuers found them dead.

Allen was placed in the home of farmer Israel Hicks, and Dr. Thomas Brushfield was shuttled from St. Mary's to St. Agnes on the St. Mary's lifeboat to attend to him. Allen was then apparently the sole survivor.

Pilot Billy Cook Hicks had died entangled in the wreckage. He left a widow and nine children.

At about 2:30 Saturday afternoon, the *Slippen* crew set out again to search for more survivors, this time rowing to the rock reef to the West of Annet called Hellweathers. At about 4:00, just before dark, Israel Hicks spotted two men on the

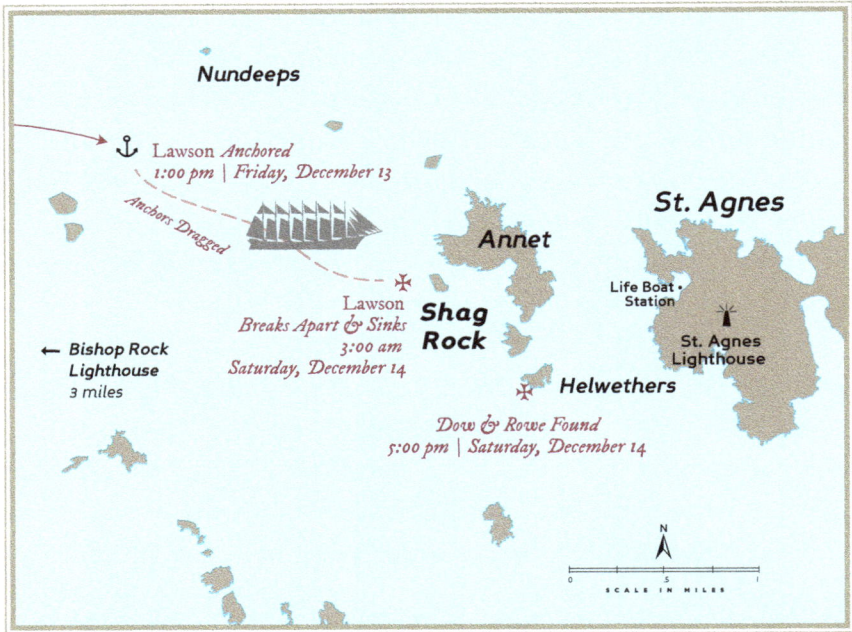

Despite her anchors, the *Lawson* is pushed by surging wind and sea onto Shag Rock, breaking up and sinking during the night and spilling her crew and oil cargo into the sea.

southern carn of Hellweathers, to the surprise of the crew who had not seen the bodies earlier in the day. William Trenary believed that they must have been out of sight in the morning, sleeping in clefts in the rock. The crew noticed Engineer Rowe when he waved Captain Dow's mackintosh. It took about an hour of maneuvering for the gig to get close enough to throw a rope to Rowe. After many failed attempts, Rowe was able to reach out and grab the rope as it fell by.

Captain Dow was the other man on Hellweathers. The crew told Rowe to tie the rope around the Captain so they could pull him out, but Rowe knew that Dow was so badly injured he would not make it to the boat alive. "Leave him there for now," Rowe shouted, "for I have secured him well." Tying a loop of rope over his head, under his arms and around his body, Rowe was persuaded to jump into the sea, allowing the *Slippen* crew to pull him aboard. Trenary said that "the groans and cries of that man as he was dragged through the sea" remained in his memory forever. Rowe was badly battered and had swallowed salt water and oil. Despite the pounding surf, they got Rowe back to St. Agnes, and he was helped ashore by Israel and Fred Hicks, who then took him, too, to Israel's cottage. He had been on Hellweathers for about 12 hours.

Rowe, Captain Dow, the Mate, a Steward, and Pilot Hicks had been lashed in the aft rigging when that mast fell. Rowe and the Captain had managed to jump to the deck and were washed separately overboard but clear of the wreck and onto Hellweathers, about half a mile off Annet.

The *Slippen* put out again to rescue the Captain, who was in danger of being washed off the rock. This time out, Isaac Legg and Albert Hicks replaced Israel and Fred Hicks, who looked after Rowe on St. Agnes.

Unable to land, and trying another way to reach the Captain, four men managed to get from the *Slippen* onto a brow of rocks two or three hundred yards from Captain Dow. But, after climbing over the slippery, seaweed-covered rocks to within some 20 to 25 yards of the man, they were chagrined to discover a deep gully, with seas like a "boiling cauldron, between them and the Captain." Freddie Cook Hicks—son of the pilot who had gone aboard the *Lawson* the night before and was lost in the wreck—volunteered to swim and take a rope across the gully.

"Fastening a rope around himself, he jumped in and was tossed about like a cork, but he eventually" managed to get across. Although a much smaller man than Captain Dow, who was virtually helpless from his broken wrist, other injuries and exposure, Freddie Cook got the Captain across the rock and down to the gully. The crew than dragged them by the rope across the surging current in the gully. With two men supporting each side of the Captain, they made their way back across the reef to the *Slippen* in near darkness and a rapidly rising tide, and then back to St. Agnes late in the evening, getting on 7:00 p.m..

As the *Times of London* summarized, "The captain was helpless, and of the four men who attempted the rescue, Hicks alone could swim."

They took Captain Dow to Israel's cottage in Lower Town St. Agnes, where Allen and Rowe were sheltered, and Dr. Brushfield again took the St. Mary's lifeboat across to St. Agnes to attend to him.

THE AFTERMATH

SUNDAY

S UNDAY MORNING found the St. Mary's lifeboat and many gigs from the different islands searching the rocks for

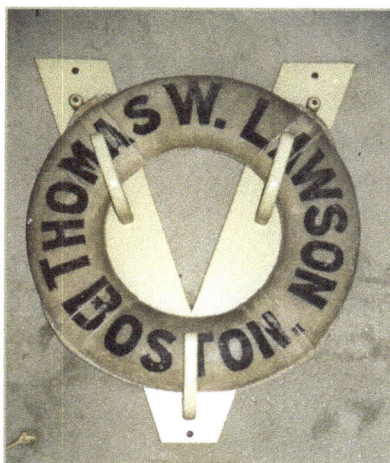

One of the *Lawson's* life preservers floated ashore

traces of other men from the *Lawson*. They recovered a head-less body—believed to be one of the officers—and, later, a fifth body that could not be identified.

With "all his ribs smashed into his lungs," severe shock and massive internal injuries, Allen died on Sunday afternoon—to no surprise of Dr. Brushfield—leaving Captain Dow and Engineer Rowe as the only survivors.

Also on Sunday, a Lloyd's insurance special surveyor named Robertson made his way from Penzance on the Western Marine Salvage Company's boat, *Lady of the Isles*, to inspect the position and condition of the *Lawson*. The ship was not insured. Also aboard was a well-known wreck salvager, named Captain Anderson. They discovered that at high tide, there was no visible trace of the schooner. And, there was no wreckage worth salvaging. Even at low tide the next day, Monday, only 15 feet of the vessel was visible.

In all, five bodies were recovered, but only three could be identified, those of Mark Sanson, the cabin boy from Brooklyn; Gustav Bohnke, the seaman from Berlin; and, supposedly, a Victor Hansell, from Sweden, although there was no record of his being on board, and this name may refer to the "Z. Olanssen" listed as a crew member.

Of the crew of 18, only two survived and 16 were lost.

INQUEST AND INQUIRY

WITHOUT DELAY, a coroner's inquest on the recovered bodies was held on Monday, December 16, 1907, at the Israel Hicks house on St. Agnes, partly because Captain Dow and Engineer Rowe were laid up there. The inquest was conducted by five men: Mr. W.M. Gluyas, the Scilly coroner; Mr. Lt. T.A. Dorrien Smith, Governor of the Isles; Mr. E.J. Bluett of the RNLI; Mr. Thomas Bradley, divisional coastguard officer; and Mr. Harold Sandrey, representing the American consul.

Several important issues were discussed at the inquest, the first being why both lifeboats left the *Lawson*, never to return. The St. Mary's lifeboat returned to its home base at about 7:30 p.m. with a broken mast and also, at the *Lawson*'s captain's instructions, to wire Falmouth for tugs. The weather was prohibitive, as the wind had shifted to northwest and had increased to a force 10 in squalls. And, they believed the St. Agnes boat was still standing by the schooner, so, they stayed ashore.

As far as the *Charles Deere James* is concerned, she had left the *Lawson* to save William Francis Hicks' life, and because the captain and pilot had refused to abandon ship and had agreed to show a light if assistance was needed. The ship had still been riding light. Having returned to St. Agnes at 9:00 p.m., with the wind blowing at force 9 and increasing, the weather made it nearly impossible to launch again, anyway. And, the pilot showed no light.

When the ship's light disappeared at about 2:50 in the morning, the witnesses said it was common for vessels' lights to be blown out. Even the coastguard officer, when informed that the ship's lights were gone, had believed that the captain had taken up the anchors and sailed westward. When asked if he thought either lifeboat could have reached the *Lawson* during the night, Officer Bradley replied, "I don't think it possible for any boat to have lived in that sea and wind, either under oars or sail."

This watch was recently brought from the *Lawson* wreck site. It was Swiss-made after 1860, but we do not know which member of the crew owned it.

The point was made that, in future such situations, better "understanding" between the St. Mary's and St. Agnes boats stations would be needed, so that each knows the other's status and does not assume that the other is responding sufficiently. In this instance, "one was depending upon the other, and then no one went."

A second issue prominent at the inquest was why the captain did not believe the *Lawson* to be in trouble for so long. He responded that he had requested and taken a pilot aboard when he found he was among islands. He had "no doubt of the ship's safety," as the anchors, weighing five tons each, would "hold her anywhere." After the tide turned, he thought they were quite safe, and told the jurors "the pilot and he were both of the same mind." He could not understand the cables or anchors giving way.

The jury expressed its admiration for the exceedingly good work of the lifeboats, and for the exceedingly brave work of the men who saved the captain and the engineer—especially Freddie Cook Hicks.

Two days later, on Wednesday, an inquiry was held at St. Mary's, regarding the loss of lifeboat man Billy Cook Hicks, with the Island's governor, Mr. Dorrien Smith, presiding. The case was discussed fully again, focusing on similar issues. They concluded that "everything that could be done was done by the lifeboats," and that precautions had already been taken to ensure that communications between the two lifeboats would not be omitted in the future.

Lieutenant Rowley, the district inspecting officer of the RNLI, was asked to recommend to the Institution that Freddie Cook Hicks be presented with an RNLI medal, in view of his rescue of Captain Dow, "at great personal risk and with marked heroism." The committee also voted condolences to the widow and family of lost pilot Billy Cook Hicks, and asked the RNLI to consider compensation for the widow.

A HYMN FOR THOSE IN PERIL ON THE SEA

THE HYMN *Eternal Father, Strong to Save* was written as a poem in 1860 by William Whiting in Winchester, England, for a student who was about to sail to the United States.

The following year, fellow Englishman Rev. John B. Dykes—an Episcopalian clergyman and organist—composed the melody. He called the hymn 'Melita', a Biblical reference to the island Malta, reached by the Apostle Paul after his ship went down.

In America, the hymn is considered the 'Navy Hymn', sung at the Naval Academy and at other ceremonies. It is also sung on ships of the British Royal Navy.

Eternal Father was the favorite hymn of President Franklin Roosevelt, a former Secretary of the Navy, and was sung at his funeral in Hyde Park, New York, in April 1945. The Navy Band played it in 1963, as President John Kennedy's body was carried up the steps of the U.S. Capitol to lie in state. Kennedy was a PT boat commander in World War II.

THE ORIGINAL FOUR VERSES

Eternal Father, strong to save,
Whose arm hath bound
    the restless wave,
Who bidd'st the mighty ocean deep
Its own appointed limits keep;
Oh, hear us when we cry to Thee,
For those in peril on the sea!

O Christ! Whose voice the waters heard
And hushed their raging at Thy word,
Who walked'st on the foaming deep,
And calm amidst its rage didst sleep;
Oh, hear us when we cry to Thee,
For those in peril on the sea!

Most Holy Spirit! Who didst brood
Upon the chaos dark and rude,
And bid its angry tumult cease,
And give, for wild confusion, peace;
Oh, hear us when we cry to Thee,
For those in peril on the sea!

O Trinity of love and power!
Our brethren shield in danger's hour;
From rock and tempest, fire and foe,
Protect them wheresoe'er they go;
Thus evermore shall rise to Thee
Glad hymns of praise from
    land and sea.

FUNERALS

O N T U E S D A Y, December 17, two funeral services were held for five victims of the wreck that were recovered. At noon, the chaplain of the islands, Reverend J.E. Sedgwick, conducted a service at the church in St. Mary's for Victor Hansell and the decapitated unidentified body. Six uniformed coastguards and two lighthouse keepers were pallbearers. English and American flags were flown at half-mast in many parts of town. The two were buried in the churchyard, placed in the same grave as some of the victims of the liner *Schiller,* which had been lost in 1875.

Later in the afternoon, the vicar of St. Agnes, the Reverend H.V. Hulbert, conducted services for cabin boy Mark Sanson, German seaman Gustav Bohnke, and another, unknown body, whom Rowe identified as a native of Nova Scotia. Reverend Hulbert delivered an eloquent requiem, and nearly all the islands' residents attended.

TWO MORE VICTIMS

O N W E D N E S D A Y, two more bodies were recovered on the southern end of Annet, evidently washed in by the southwest wind. One was nude, with tattoos on the arms, including the letters "J.A.P.," perhaps Petersen. The other man was partly dressed, but with nothing to help identify him. They were left at Annet until coffins could be brought from St. Mary's.

In all, eight bodies were recovered, and the American government provided eight coffins.

THE CAPTAIN

CAPTAIN DOW spent about six weeks recuperating in the St. Agnes home of Israel and Charlotte Hicks, where Dr. Brushfield would visit from St. Mary's. His injuries comprised a broken arm, wrist, and two ribs. (The Ellsworth newspaper commented a few days after the wreck that "Had he not weighed 250 pounds, he would perhaps not have survived.")

When told the news that he and Rowe were the only survivors, "he was greatly affected." On Sunday, December 15, with considerable understatement, he pronounced, "The experience that I have been through the last forty-eight hours is something that I never want to go through again."

He was too ill to attend the inquest that was held, but told the coroner that he considered his cables would hold his ship in any gale he had experienced on the American coast.

Dow's wife—an invalid at home in Melrose—and son Richard had received early word of the wreck and the presumption that all aboard had been lost. In the first message "flashed across the wires," the captain was given up as lost. For nearly 24 hours, they had been receiving messages of condolence and sympathy. But all was reversed upon hearing the good news, and Mrs. Dow received her friends, guests, and callers showering her with their congratulations long into Monday night.

The patience and self-denial, learned through long years of illness and suspense for her husband's safety during the hundreds of voyages which he has made in the last forty years, disappeared entirely in joy at the complete reverse of the almost realized fears of the family.

In wife Jennie's own words:

> *Of course, I always have felt more or less timid when the captain leaves for a new voyage, and for several years I have tried to persuade him to stay at home and give up this life. He has tried it, but I really think it would have shortened his days. He says that he cannot breathe freely on land, he is so used to having so much room. And like all sailors, he would never say good-by when he left me for a new trip. He did not the last time, and when I first heard of the wreck, I kept thinking of this.*
>
> *I hope that this will be his last voyage, but I do not know whether he can be persuaded to remain at home or not. He will not be here at Christmas with us, but I know it will be the happiest one that I have seen in many years, when I think of his narrow escape from death and know that he did escape. I shall probably get a letter from him in a few days.*

ROWE

T HE ENGINEER, Edward Rowe, also recovered and returned to America. Having been wrecked three times previously in his sailing life, he soon worked only ashore, retiring completely more than 30 years later in 1939 at age 65.

Born in 1873 in Machias, Maine, having written his story about what happened, and having out-survived Captain Dow by four decades, Rowe was a unique source of information and perspective about the people and events of the *Lawson* and its tragic end. Particularly interesting is a long interview of 84-year-old Rowe by his nephew, Edward Rowe Snow, in January 1958. For nearly 40 years, the engineer had been the only survivor of the *Lawson* and in 1958 lived in a trailer home in Essex, Massachusetts.

Rowe apparently enjoyed being *the* authority, disagreeing with the accounts of others, and "setting the record straight." He was strong-willed and frequently disagreeable, having left one ship early in his sailing career, he admits, because he "couldn't get along with the captain."

According to his author nephew Snow, the engineer "disagreed with almost every so-called authority on what happened in 1907 to this unique schooner." Rowe said, "It is so easy to get the truth, but no one seems to bother. The old, accepted stories, all wrong, are the ones which people remember ... No one has given an accurate story as yet." With

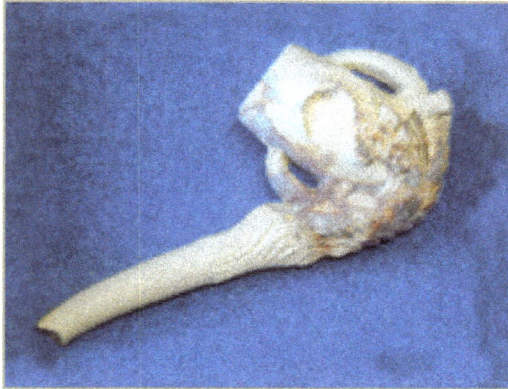

This small "eagles claw" clay pipe was found on the wreck in 2015.

all this said, his account is generally in line with others who participated at various stages of the tragedy, although even his own versions changed over the years and at times were contradictory.

THE RESCUERS

E ACH MEMBER of the *Slippen* crew was given a gold medal by the U.S. Government for the rescue work.

Freddie Cook Hicks was presented with two gold watches for courage in saving Captain Dow: One, an inscribed gold watch with chain and fob presented by the American Government for the humane and heroic rescue; and the other by the ship's owners. He had, of course, lost his father, who went down with the *Lawson* as its last pilot. Freddie Cook outlived all the other December 14 *Slippen* crew, living with his wife on St. Agnes. And, John Horace—Jack—Hicks was the last Trinity pilot in Scilly.

Elizabeth Ann, widow of the lost pilot and life boatman Billy Cook Hicks, soon moved permanently to Australia with her four youngest children, assisted by an amount of money raised by the RNLI and others on the islands.

Received, through the Department of State, Washington, *a gold watch to chain* awarded to me by the President of the United States of America, as a testimonial for services rendered by me in saving life from the American *Schooner Thomas W. Lawson*.

on the 14th. day of *December* , 1907 .

F. C Hicks.

Witness:

The receipt from Freddie Cook Hicks for the gold watch awarded by the U. S. Government for saving Captain Dow.

O VER THE FOLLOWING DECADES, it became accepted that the wreck occurred to the west of the Haycocks, outside of Minmanueth. However, the wrecked *Lawson* was relocated elsewhere in 1969. The bow rests just to the North-east of Shag Rock, the stern just to the Southwest. They are about a quarter mile apart in water about 55 feet deep. The location is 49 degrees, 53', 38" North Latitude, and 6 degrees, 22', 55" West Longitude. The area is a popular site for divers, although "windless conditions are required for diving to the wreck."

The gig *Slippen* was the smallest Scilly gig at just under 28 feet long. She had been built of elm in 1830 by the Peters company in St. Mawes. She was eventually refitted with a new English oak keel and moved to Newquay, on the English mainland. She was one of the last of the 19th century gigs in service, and retired to the museum in Newquay. She still is occasionally brought back to Scilly to participate in the summer gig racing, 185 years after her launch.

THE NAMESAKE

T HE *LAWSON*'S builder and original part owner, the busi-nessman Thomas W. Lawson, had been wronged by the Standard Oil Company on a previous Friday, the 13th. And, ear-lier in 1907, Lawson had published a book, entitled *Friday the Thirteenth*, depicting a fictional stock market crash on that date. On Friday, December 13, at their Scituate, Massachusetts, home, Thomas Lawson and his son Douglas had a long conversation, while, unbeknownst to them, the schooner *Lawson* was breaking up in Scilly. According to Douglas, the elder, highly-superstitious Lawson said, "Well, this Friday the 13th went off without anything going wrong."

Two days later, and reflecting his continuing bitterness about the power and emerging dominance of 'big oil' in the shipping trade, he wrote the following biting and sarcastic 'obituary' for the ship:

> Thomas W. Lawson *destroyed by Standard Oil on Friday, the 13th, and they say that I have written improbably things.*
>
> *'Twas an ancient, and to one of his flesh 'For gold you go to the enemy's tents, I grieve, but I send with thee my best curse.'*
>
> *The past four years they have been trying to fill me up with their oil. Despairing of success, they filled up my big name-sake, and now, realizing her prostitution, she did the only thing outraged virtue should do—purged herself at awful cost.*
>
> *This trust oil business is dirty. I've been in it and I'm striving day and night to forget it. The* Thomas W. *would never have been in it could I have prevented. I can imagine her feelings as she struggled with God's angry ocean, compelled to hear above the roar of the gale the awash of her degradation. I am sad because of the fate of her brave sailors, doubly sad for their families.*

I was the largest owner, and, therefore, the heaviest loser, but my loss does not count, as it was only dollars. Willingly would I have lost many times as much if by so doing I could put in the place of those honest sailor lads an equal number of Standard oil masters.

When I wrote 'Friday the 13th,' some said my story was improbable. I answered: Nothing in life is improbable. Mine has been a chain of improbabilities. When He selected Friday, the 13th, for the destruction of the grandest sea bird that ever floated, He must have intended it as a message; but we, sogged in our intellectuality of ignorance, cannot interpret it; at least it is another proof that the really strange things in life are not those figments of our imagination.

I had hoped that He would have marked Friday, the 13th, by lifting 26 Broadway [in New York City and known then as the Standard Oil Company Building], the City Bank and a few of the other creations of Frenzied Finance and depositing them and their contents beneath the rocks of Hell Gate, but 'He doeth all things well.'

The next year, 1908, Lawson gave up his fight against corporate misbehavior as having been ineffective, and to "allow the public to do their own reforming." He returned to the business of speculating in the stock market, "for the purpose of recouping the millions I have donated to my public work." He also published several novels.

But, his erratic personality and attacks on the 'money kings' and on many other aspects of American life eventually took their toll. He accumulated many critics, and lost his "knack for success" after about 1910. He subsequently lost his mansion and even his automobile, dying a relatively poor man in 1925.

REFLECTIONS

HUMAN ERROR

A T T H E I N Q U E S T following the tragedy, there was some criticism of the lack of cooperation between the two lifeboats. The coxswain of the *Charles Deere Jones*, from St. Agnes, said he did not communicate with the St. Mary's boat, because he thought that, with 150 fathoms of chain out, the *Lawson*'s anchors would hold, and he also had every confidence in the pilot.

However, two days after the wreck, Engineer Rowe emphasized that blame could not be placed on the Friday night rescue crews who returned to shore, "because the Captain decided to stand by the ship and do his best." When asked why no signals of distress were made, Rowe responded "That is nothing to do with me."

Mr. Bradley, district officer of the coastguards said he considered that after midnight, it would have been impossible for any lifeboat to have lived in such a sea. The tugs had started out from Falmouth, but the weather was too bad for them. Also, the tug *Lyonesse* was requested by telegraph to Penzance, but the weather stopped them from getting out as well.

Among the many contradictions or differences in recollections and opinions about the final voyage and outcome, an important one concerns whether the captain and pilot believed they were in a dire situation late Friday evening. The account of Jack Hicks quotes the Captain as clearly wanting little help, other than a pilot to come aboard and a call to be made for a tug to be dispatched, relying instead on his anchors to last through any worsening of the storm in the night. And, when the tide turned to the North and the anchors still held, pilot Billy Cook thought it would be all right, and they all went down into the cabin.

Captain Dow reported on Sunday that,

> *Time and time again they attempted to get close enough to take our men off, but the Lawson was rocking so violently that it meant sure death to them, and so after a consultation with my men we sent them back, for we preferred to take our own chances against the storm rather than to have those brave men go down.*

MISCALCULATIONS

W HICHEVER VERSION is accurate, there remain Captain Dow's two tragic mistakes: believing the light to leeward was another boat heading west instead of the Bishop Rock light that it was, and later believing his anchors would hold and therefore not abandoning ship.

Regarding mistaking the light, present-day navigation guides admonish:

> *Give these points a wide berth, and in thick weather make no attempt to sight the Bishop Rock Lighthouse,*

the Scilly Isles or the English coast until well round the Lizard [on the south mainland coast] and closing Falmouth after keeping clear of the Manacle Rocks.

Perhaps with a lack of familiarity with Scilly, and in light of days of dead reckoning and the horrendous weather and visibility, it is understandable why Captain Dow did not know his position until he was inside Broad Sound.

Regarding believing his anchors sufficient, the Captain thought that the wind would drop and that, in any case, the anchors would hold out the storm. And, pilot Hicks agreed enough to board and stay aboard. Unfortunately, according to James Thomas Hicks, the wind shifted from the west to north-northwest and blew in fierce squalls, "which accounted for the disaster."

NATURE, PHYSICS AND LUCK

IN ADDITION to the *human* errors that put the ship in its untenable position and failed to preserve the lives of the crew and pilot, *nature* was a primary contributor to the tragedy. Three weeks of fierce storms across the Atlantic had ravaged the *Lawson*. And, most important, the storms that obliterated all visibility and the ability to take navigational observations on Friday were the catalysts for the predicament and the sinking. A perfect storm did the ship in at the end, with powerful squalls and wind, a surging tide, and enormous waves snapping the two anchor chains and smashing the *Lawson* on the rocks.

The laws of *physics* played their part throughout the *Lawson's* troubled five-year life and in her final hours. The huge hull, with its length eight times its width, acted as a sail in itself—especially with less than a full load—exerting tremendous forces no matter whether canvass sails were furled, and no matter how the tiller and rudder were set. The lack of maneuverability and the tendency to blow over contributed to the various groundings and harbor mishaps over her lifetime.

Captain Dow's son Richard concluded later:

> I consider the whole life of the Lawson an experiment even to not fully loading her with oil on her last trip—a condition that did not improve her sea-worthiness by any means. The lamentable fact is that 17 men were lost under conditions that could possibly have been avoided if the ship had been manageable.

Finally, there is *luck*, which ran out on the *Lawson*, but not as much on the Captain. Some point out that the lucky number of seven masts kept her profitable and protected until the year 1907. But, she has 13 letters in her name, and she reputedly had had 13 accidents during her five-year life prior to the final trip. Adding to that, her namesake and partial owner had published the book earlier that same year, entitled *Friday the Thirteenth*. As a result, she had become known as an unlucky vessel, and finding herself struck by 'terminal' conditions on Friday the 13th, she succumbed.

Captain Dow, on the other hand, was known as a lucky Captain long before the voyage on the *Lawson*. In an era when most ocean going sailing vessels—especially wooden ones—met their ends on reefs or in storms, fires, or collisions, Captain Dow by 1907 had mastered many vessels across the seas for nearly 40 years. At age 60, and although devastated in many ways by the events of December 13 and 14, 1907, he had survived.

A later observation about the *Lawson*'s demise finds it

> *Curious, that in her dying this greatest of all sailing ships should have orchestrated so many of the elements that make the sea forever alluring to those who follow it: superstition, storm, life-or-death decision, shipwreck, tragedy, and, like the silver peal of a bugle, heroism.*

As with other sea tragedies—including, for example, the sinking of the *Titanic* in 1912, and Sir Ernest Shackleton's abandoning the *Endurance* in Antarctica in 1914-15—a combination of nature, human error, physics, and luck are to blame for the event and its results. In the cases of the *Lawson* and *Titanic*, there were many deaths and few survivors; in the case of the *Endurance*, not a single life was lost.

When a vessel is lost and the Captain survives, eyebrows naturally are raised with reference to the age-old maxim that "the captain always goes down with the ship." In the case of the *Lawson*'s demise, the Captain and Engineer were the only survivors. But, even if a Captain's self-sacrifice was an ethical imperative in past centuries, most would argue that such a moral obligation is not—and never was—justified, no matter how egregious or negligent actions on the part of the Captain, and no matter how great the resulting loss of life or property. The ethicist Chuck Klosterman, for example, concludes:

> To remain on a boat while it sinks into the sea ... is not a reasonable job expectation. The value of a ship itself is not greater than the value of the person controlling it. Even if the Captain's own negligence results in hundreds of deaths, it's not his symbolic duty to add his life to the total. If he's no longer in a position to save anyone else, he can absolutely save himself.

A PLACE IN HISTORY

THE SHIPWRECK of the *Thomas W. Lawson* was significant to the Scilly's and in the world of oil transportation and environmental damage. Of the estimated 900 ships that were wrecked in Scilly's waters, the *Lawson* was the largest on record until the 1920's.

The *Lawson* had become a total loss in 15 minutes. Immediately and for two days, the stench of 6,500 tons of oil filled the water and air around the whole of the islands. It was the world's first major oil spill.

Over the next 60 years, "conservationist and pollution experts ... viewed with alarm the increase in size of oil tankers and could only theorise on the effect of one of the huge craft being wrecked and spilling its cargo on the sea."

The inevitable happened in March 1967, with the largest-ever shipwreck near Scilly. The 974-foot long, 61,000-ton supertanker *Torrey Canyon* wrecked on Pollard Rock at Seven Stones reef, seven miles northeast of St. Martin's, "while trying to take a shortcut round Lands End." The spill of nearly 120,000 tons of crude oil dwarfed the *Lawson's*, and the slick covered an area 35 miles by 20 miles. The waves took the oil to the east, away from the Scilly Isles, but 180 miles of shoreline in England and France suffered instead.

The supertanker *Torrey Canyon* breaks apart on Pollard Rock in 1967.

In 2000, the East African country of Djibouti issued an attractive postage stamp featuring the *Lawson* at full sail. Interestingly, the stamp collector community (philatelists) categorizes the stamp as "Tankershipping."

Besides the Djibouti stamp, a set of gold and silver commemorative coins was issued in 2001 by another African country, the Republic of Congo, also showing the *Lawson* under full sail.

THE *LAWSON* left Philadelphia on its trans-Atlantic cross-ing to London just as the new Cunard liner *Mauretania* was half way through its maiden Atlantic crossing going in the opposite direction, from Liverpool to New York. Pow-ered by the first steam turbines used in a passenger vessel, the *Mauretania* took five days and five hours to make the crossing, from November 16 to the 22nd. The *Lawson* took 24 days—more than four times as long—despite being only half as long and one-third as heavy as the *Mauretania*, and having the prevailing westerly winds at her back. Although running into fog and storms, herself, the *Mauretania* averaged twenty-five miles per hour, the *Lawson* six. The *Mauretania* soon set the speed record for Atlantic crossings in both directions and held the records and their Blue Ribands for the next 20 years. That a ship of such size could achieve so great a speed was considered one of the miracles of the modern age.

On her maiden Atlantic crossing from Liverpool to New York,
R. M. S. Mauretania takes five days against the winds, compapred
to the *Lawson*'s time of 24 days, sailing with the wind to her back.

Two days after the loss of the *Lawson*, the *New York Times* wrote:

> *The wreck of the* Lawson *has occasioned some newspaper discussion on the advisability of building such enormous vessels. Although the papers grant that she had safely weathered the dangerous Atlantic passage, they believe that owing to the disaster no more such many masted schooners are likely to be built.*

None were, and there was good reason. Coastwise, for example, had concentrated on using coastal schooners with simple designs and multiple masts that could be operated cheaply. The company owned nine multi-masted vessels, including the *Lawson*. Overall, they "were a disaster. Unwieldy and of marginal seaworthiness, the vessels were wrecked one by one." In 1908, the Treasurer of Coastwise wrote to the stockholders "the common stock is absolutely valueless. As you are well aware, the past year has been a disastrous one for this company, the loss of the schooner *Thomas W. Lawson* and other vessels has seriously crippled us ..."

Far beyond Coastwise, incrementally better use of technology—that is, more masts and longer, narrower hulls for more speed and smaller crews—"was reaching its natural limit, and the end of the sailing ship era was near." In fact, four hundred years earlier, Columbus had found the fore-and-aft sail rigging unsatisfactory for the open ocean, having added square sail to the fore-and-aft rig on the *Nina*.

On the day the *Lawson* was launched in 1902, Thomas A.

Watson, the founder and President of its builder, the Fore River Ship and Engine Building Company, said to a reporter:

> *Such ships as these, with their many masts and consequent tremendous sail power, which makes it possible to carry immense cargoes at a comparatively low cost, are going to do much toward reestablishing the supremacy of American shipping on the seas.*

Watson was correct about the coming transformation of shipping, but wrong that sail power would drive it. Steam and turbines soon led the way. (Before founding the Fore River company, Watson had been in the forefront of an earlier transformative technology, working as Alexander Graham Bell's assistant in inventing the telephone and receiving the first call—"Mr. Watson ... come here ... I want you.")

In the two decades following the wreck of the *Lawson*, particularly after World War I, the multi-masted schooners rapidly gave way to large steamships at sea, and to the railroads and trucking on land, in transporting bulk cargo in the United States and around the world. ⚓

PART 5

Toward Retirement

*The Captain retires in Melrose, breaking his family line
from both Maine and seafaring, as his descendants pursue
other occupations across America.*

RECUPERATION

C APTAIN DOW remained at Israel Hicks's home on St.
Agnes for nearly six weeks, under the care of Israel's wife
Charlotte, assisted by her sister Agnes.

At the end of January 1908, the Captain left the Hicks home
to return to the United States on the American Line steamship *SS Philadelphia*, crossing from Southampton to New York.
(Just six months before, Orville Wright had crossed on the
Philadelphia from New York to La Havre, France, accompanied
by his newest (disassembled) airplane *The Flyer III*, to join his
brother Wilbur in negotiations to sell the plane to the French
military.)

Six weeks into recuperation, Captain Dow returns to
the U.S. on the American Line steamship *Philadelphia,*
arriving in New York harbor on February 2, 1908.

Captain Dow arrived in New York harbor on February 2, and then went on to Boston by train, and finally to his home in Melrose, to continue his recuperation with Jennie.

In October of that year, he received the postcard from his sister Rose in Maine, and, presumably soon thereafter, the potatoes she had sent.

Picture post cards seem to have been a medium of choice for communications among the Captain's family—especially between 1906 and 1910. These cards were sent from myriad locations in the northeastern U.S., California, and elsewhere, to the Captain and Jennie in Melrose. Jennie created two additional albums of picture postcards—most never posted and without messages—corresponding to places of interest around her homes, and from California to Maine.

A LITTLE MORE SAILING

THE *CALUMET*

AFTER A "DOMESTIC YEAR" of recuperation during the rest of 1908, Captain Dow was at sea again in 1909, having taken command of the four-masted schooner *Calumet*, owned by the Emery's and sailing out of Boston. The *Calumet* weighed in at 1,241 tons, the largest vessel Dow commanded except for the Lawson. Built in 1900 in Bath, Maine, the *Calumet* was 190 feet by 40 feet by 19 feet draught.

George W. Dow returns to sea in 1909 as captain of the four-masted schooner *Calumet*.

THE *INEZ N. CARVER*

IN 1910, the Captain moved on again and was master of the schooner *Inez N. Carver*, built at Bath in 1901, and overhauled in 1908. Owned by A.H. Bull & Co., and sailing out of the port of New York, she weighed 730 tons and was 167 feet by 36 feet by 13 feet.

In 1910, Captain Dow becomes master of his last vessel,
the *Inez N. Carver*, a four-masted
schooner shown here on launch day in 1901.

On November 5, 1910, the following account of the *Inez N. Carver* appeared in *The Bath Daily Times:*

> *One of the overdue vessels for the safety of which much anxiety is felt is the schooner* Inez N. Carver, *which sailed from Mobile on Oct. 1 for Baltimore, and is supposed to have been in the path of the recent hurricane. Several wrecks have been passed similar in size to the*

Carver. *The schooner was in command of Capt. Dow, who was in the seven-master* Thomas W. Lawson *when she was lost on the English coast.*

Indeed, the *Carver* had sailed with a cargo of lumber on a trip that normally took 12 to 15 days, but had encountered the "West India hurricane" off the Florida keys in mid-October and had put out to sea to avoid going ashore.

However, on November 12, the Newport News *Daily Press* reported:

> *Nearly a month overdue, the schooner* Inez Carver, *badly battered, arrived here today ... The experience, according to Captain Dow, was one of the most thrilling that the crew has ever made.*

Alas, both the *Carver* and her master survived that storm.

A final group of undocumented or unconfirmed "mentions" that might or might not have involved our Captain Dow during his sailing career includes a schooner named *Everglade* or *Everglades,* a bark *Colorado,* and another schooner named *Bark*. Although these have been cited in passing by various family descendants, no details of any kind have been found, including any dates, places, or information about the vessels. And, no Dow is listed as captain of any vessels with these names.

After Captain Dow retires from the sea in 1910 at the age of 63, he and Jennie remain in their Melrose home where they had lived since 1886.

MELROSE RETIREMENT

SHORTLY AFTER the two brief stints on the *Calumet* and *Inez N. Carver*, Captain Dow retired for good in 1910, living in Melrose at age 63. He remained an avid cribbage player, as were many sea captains of the time, and he no doubt spent many hours in retirement at the cribbage board. Meanwhile, son Orville was living with his own family in East Boston, not far from Melrose.

Late in 1908, his son Richard (mostly "Dick") moved west to Contra Costa County, California, just east of San Francisco, to work in the chemical industry. Dick and Annie Dinnie, his fiancé, virtually eloped, and it is unclear if they married before or after leaving Massachusetts. Dick sent his mother a post card from Pueblo, Colorado, on his cross-country drive to his new job and home. It said:

Dear mother—
A great ride—lots of beautiful sights—long but not tire-
some

—Dick

From the Dow arrival in the New World in 1637, no one from Captain Dow's lineage had lived west or south of Boston until the Captain's son Dick moved to California in 1908, nine generations and 270 years later.

In California, Dick worked for the General Chemical Company of California in the town of Bay Point and by 1917 had become General Superintendent and Factory Manager. He lived two miles down the road in Nichols, part of the town of Martinez, with a population of about 600, where in 1923 he was also the Manager General, or mayor, as well as Deputy Sheriff of Contra Costa County.

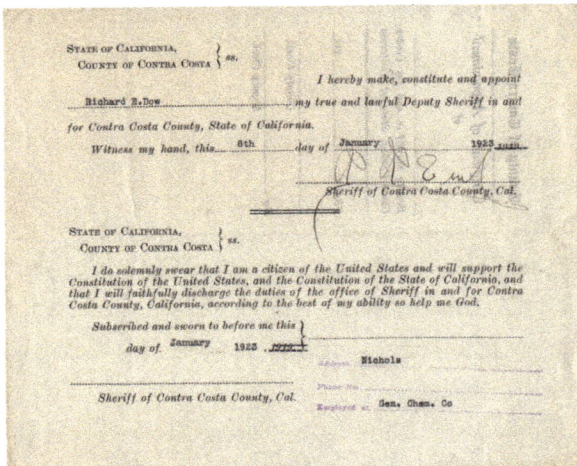

Dick's appointment as Deputy Sheriff of Contra Costa County, 1923

As the local Melrose newspaper wryly observed about Dick's activities and success in California:

> *He surely is a busy man, and he knew how to blow his own horn when in Melrose, he seems to manage a whole orchestra now.*

After a long day of work at the plant and for the town, Dick milked his cows, fed the chickens, did a little gardening, and played music with his children: Richard E., born in October 1909 and who died at age three or four, most likely from the influenza and pneumonia or tuberculosis epidemics that hit the San Francisco area in the winters of 1912 and 1913; Anne D., born in June 1914; Richard B. (also "Dick"), born in January 1916; and the youngest, Mary, born in May 1920.

A note written in 1923 by the Captain's seven-year-old grandson Richard (Dick's son Dick) to his father ("daddy") indicates that the Captain's wife Jennie still played the disciplinarian role. "Grandma" is Jennie, "Annie" and "Mary" are young Richard's younger sisters, and "Josie" is his young cousin:

> *Dear daddy.*
> *How are you. I am fine.*
> *Grandma and Josie and annie and mama blame every-*
> *thing on me.*
> *My wagon is fine. Josie gave mary the doll buggy.*
> *I had a tooth ache Thursday and Friday all day. I didn't*
> *go to school.*
> *Grandma slaped my face yesterday and called me a girl*
> *and I don't like her.*

And annie called me a girl, and annie is a god dam fool,
and I don't like her.
  Your friend, Richard

GIRARD'S BIZARRE SAGA

I N 1917, "adopted son" Girard Graves split with wife Rebecca Lewis Pratt Graves and returned to Maine, leaving her and the two youngest children in Boston.

Girard went to live in a cottage on the shore at Franklin Bay, on the Taunton River near the lobster pound in Hancock. The cottage was positioned so he could see the tide rips through an opening in the surrounding fir trees. His aunt Amelia had bought the property, and when she died in 1921, it passed to her sister, Girard's mother Ernestine, who had been living there. But, Ernestine moved to live with her brother Erwin in Shirley, Maine, and Girard lived in "Bushe Cottege" for more than four decades until his death in 1959, having rebuilt it following a fire in 1920.

Over those decades, Girard made do with odd jobs and with his hobbies of hunting, fishing and preaching. During the 1920's, for example, he conducted trout and salmon fishing trips and big and small game hunts. He also worked for the power company, clearing land for the power lines coming to Hancock for the first time. In 1933, he painted the inside of the Hancock Falls schoolhouse, and in 1936, at age 66, he was working at the Mount Desert Ferry.

Margaret Chase Smith, Maine's long-time senator, visited

"Bushe Cottege" on the Taunton River in Hancock, where Girard lived alone for nearly 40 years until his death in 1959.

Girard at his home in Hancock, having evidently developed a lively acquaintanceship by mail.

Girard remained an avid hunter and fisherman well into his 80's, and he would send fox and other fashionable furs from his hunting successes to Captain Dow's son Richard's wife Annie in Hamburg, New York.

During many years preceding Girard's death in 1959 at age 90, Richard would drive to Hancock from his home in Hamburg, to pay the property tax on Girard's home directly to the long-time local treasurer, Lura Crabtree.

In 1906, a Boston doctor had told Girard, then 36 years old, that he had but two years to live. Girard almost certainly out-lived the doctor, despite being a lifelong smoker.

In 1918, only a year after Rebecca Graves and Girard split and

At age 83, 'adopted son' Girard Graves prepares his 20-gauge shotgun for the 1952 hunting season in Hancock County, 46 years after a doctor told him he had two years to live.

Girard returned to Maine, Rebecca died of heart trouble in Boston. The three children apparently were already living with other relatives, Mildred (24 years old and not yet married) with her Pratt grandparents, and the younger Lewis and Harriet with cousins.

The Graves' children grew up believing that their father Girard had died in 1917, and an insurance policy on Girard's life, paid to their mother, seemed to confirm this. As a result, Girard's children had no clue that their father was still very much alive.

In 1995, Girard's granddaughter was doing genealogical research about her ancestors and telephoned Lois Johnson at the Historical Society in Hancock. She asked Lois if the Historical Society might have any information about her grandfather, Girard Graves, even though she knew he had died way back in 1917. After an awkward pause, Lois told the woman that Girard had not passed away until 1959, and that she remembered him in Hancock very well. Only then did the granddaughter and her family discover that Girard had lived in Hancock for 42 years, unbeknownst to any of them.

Girard's cottage looked over the Taunton River tidal 'rapids' that ripple when the tide is both coming in and going out.

PASSING OF THE CAPTAIN'S FAMILY

IN SEPTEMBER OF 1916, the Captain and Jennie's first son Orville died at his home at 23 Monmouth Street in East Boston, at the age of only 45. He left wife Hazel, fourteen-year-old son George, and nine-year-old daughter Josephine. Orville had remained a pharmacist on Brookline Street in Boston. He was buried in the family plot in McFarland Hill Cemetery, Hancock, next to his brother and sister who had died in their childhoods. Although Orville is buried in Hancock, his family is not and had little connection with the Maine communities or the Richard Dow ancestors or descendants.

The Captain is buried in Lot 41 of McFarland Hill Cemetery in Hancock, joined there by Jennie and children Orville, Ellery, and Georgie. Girard Graves is also buried in the plot.

On Monday, March 17, 1919, Captain George W. Dow died at home in Melrose, at age 71. His wife Jennie and son Richard, in from California, were at his bedside.

The Captain may have never fully recovered his health from the ordeal in Scilly. His obituary in the local newspaper indicates simply that he died at home following an illness.

Funeral services were held at home on Wednesday, March 19, with the Captain's former pastor in Melrose, the Reverend Thomas J. Horner, coming from his Unitarian church in Manchester, New Hampshire, to officiate. The Captain is buried in Lot 41 of McFarland Hill Cemetery at Hancock.

The Captain's wife, Jennie Bush Dow had been ill for many years but lived on at home in Melrose for another 12 years. She died of cancer in 1931, but it is not known if the cancer is what inflicted her for three decades. She was 84 years old and is buried in McFarland Cemetery with her husband and three of their children.

The Captain's surviving son Richard died of cancer at age 82 in August 1961, at Hamburg, New York. He had moved from California to company management positions at Allied Chemical's General Chemical subsidiary in Pittsburg (1924), Chicago, New York City, and Cleveland. In 1927, Richard moved from 2304 Roanoke Avenue in Cleveland, to Hamburg, a Buffalo suburb, where he rented a house at 27 Central Avenue, and then another at 46 Prospect Avenue. Sometime before 1934, he bought the house at 50 North Street, where he would live the last three decades of his life with his wife Annie. This was the first and only house he had actually owned.

Following his retirement in 1946, Richard continued to play his cornet at home and loved his cribbage, an interest—and a board—he had inherited from his seafaring father. Richard's grandson, William Dow Turner, recalls visiting 50 North Street in Hamburg as a boy and being well aware of the cribbage board, pipe cabinet, planter's chair, cuspidor, and ostrich eggs, all handed down from Captain Dow. A fine top hat—reputedly presented to the Captain by the government of Puerto Rico—remains with the family. There were also two

oddities Richard kept in his bedroom—an unloaded Derrin-
ger pistol resting on a small set of antlers on the wall above
the bed, and his pickled appendix in a jar on a dresser.

Richard was the first of his line not to be buried in the Hancock family plot. Wife Annie lived near son Richard's family
in Tennessee until she died in January 1970, and she is buried
with her husband in Forrest Lawn Cemetery in Buffalo. ⚓

Epilogue

A Change of Course

H ENRY DOW reset the course for future generations of his descendants by pivoting away from 17th century England and bringing his family to America. Eight generations later, George W. Dow reset the course once again, by moving his family from small-town Maine to cosmopolitan Boston, to maintain his seafaring career.

Although the Captain and Jennie maintained close relationships and business dealings with siblings and their families back in Maine, and although both are buried in the family plot there, never again did they own property in the state or consider their home to be other than in Melrose, Massachusetts.

The couple transitioned from families of 10 Dow and 12 Bush siblings, to their own family of two surviving sons. One son stayed in Boston, died young with two children, and is buried in the family plot in Hancock. The other son moved west, had three surviving children, and worked and lived in six different states before dying at age 82 and being buried in Buffalo.

Sons Orville and Richard were the first generation in Captain Dow's line to attend college, and to abandon the Maine farming and seafaring legacies for professional careers elsewhere. They were the first in four generations not to be sea captains.

The Dows lived comfortably in Melrose, owned their own house, and upon their deaths left possessions and money of modest value to their heirs. They appear to have been church-going but without the strict Puritan and German religious practices of their families' forbearers.

THE CAPTAIN AS CAPTAIN

CAPTAIN DOW was a master at sailing, in both senses of the word. For nearly 45 years, he sailed square-riggers and schooners from Hancock and Boston to ports across the Western Hemisphere. His sailing and leadership skills were praised by crews, and were recognized by the Emery firm and other owners, who kept him employed steadily through the decades. Those skills and his record were known to the Crowleys of Coastwise Transportation, who chose him to take the giant and unique *Thomas W. Lawson* across the Atlantic for the first time. This voyage proved to be the pinnacle of Captain Dow's notoriety as a captain, but also his biggest challenge and sole disaster.

Misjudging his position approaching Scilly, and then failing to abandon ship, proved to be the undoing of the *Lawson* and its crew. Nevertheless, surviving the wreck allowed Captain Dow to retire from the sea several years later and to sustain his label as a "lucky captain," having narrowly escaped with his own life. He outlived virtually all his vessels—and their logbooks.

THE CAPTAIN AS A MAN

GEORGE DOW was also dedicated and successful beyond his seafaring career. Although there is very little record of his spoken word—and even less of any writings—we can infer a bit. From his chosen profession and his lifelong sailing record, it is clear that he took pleasure and satisfaction in being in charge and responsible, but also from being largely alone at sea for weeks and months at a time. Aboard ship, he had his pipes, his cribbage set, and his conversation, all of which we assume he used with his crews, during the many hours of clear sailing with little sailing work to be done. And, we assume that he took full advantage of the onboard book libraries whenever available on his vessels.

Beyond the decks and staterooms of his vessels, however, we do not know the extent of his interest in or curiosity about the ports, people, and histories of the many places he visited. We have no record of any interest or proficiency with foreign languages. And, other than a few souvenirs and gifts from crews and others abroad, there is no record of his experiences or observations in those far-flung places, where he cumulatively spent many years.

We do know that he was a "family man," to at least a significant extent. His apparently strong and sustained relationships with Jennie and their two sons, his sending both sons to college, his taking in and "raising" Girard Graves, and his continued interactions with family members back in Hancock point to a sincere effort to maintain a healthy and prosperous family life.

There are no records of family vacations, exotic travel, or significant holiday events, but with the Captain away sailing much of the time, this would be understandable.

Regarding his personality, including the warmth and nature of relationships with his wife and sons, there are few first-hand sources to shed much light. Stoic he was. The captain's few written comments and oral quotes by others demonstrate that he was well-spoken, direct, to the point, and respectful, but they do not reveal inner thoughts, feelings, or sensitivities. For example, T.C. Moon's quotes of Captain Dow in his description of events on the *Stampede* contain tinges of headstrong competence and calm but firm direction—seemingly appropriate for the situation. Moon says that the captain "could tell a good story" and did so, but that is as revealing as it gets. The Captain's note to the American Seamen's Friend Society regarding borrowed books is a rare personal message, and it expresses sincere thanks and a bit of contrition on his part.

Despite dozens of post cards written to and from Jennie and other family members between 1895 and 1915—including some to the Captain—there is not a single one written *by* the Captain.

Later, in testimony and quoted conversations following the wreck of the *Lawson* in England, the captain expresses himself with sincerity and humility about the catastrophe, and he lucidly describes his recollection of events that night and the next morning. But, over the next, and last, 11 years of his life, there is not a single sentence or thought attributed to him, relating to the *Lawson* episode or his four-decade sailing career. And, we have no evidence that he ever contacted any member of the Hicks family—or anyone else in Scilly—after his return to Boston in 1908. It is unclear if this reflects his innately private personality, some degree of guilt or embarrassment about his role in the tragedy, or merely an aversion to writing. ⚓

BIBLIOGRAPHY

A History of the Town of Hancock 1828-1978. Hancock, ME: The Town of Hancock, 1978.

"A Scilly Question." *Conde Naste Traveler.* New York: Conde Naste Publications, 2001.

Allen, Philip (Editor). *The Atlantic Crossing Guide.* London: Adlard Coles, 1988.

American Lloyds Register of American and Foreign Shipping. New York, 1859-83.

Bartender, Brown Palace Hotel, Denver, Colorado. Description relating to a model of the *Thomas W. Lawson* on display, 1974.

Bastable, Jonathan. "Remotely British." *Conde Naste Traveller.* New York: Conde Naste Publications, July, 2004.

Bath Daily Times, Bath, ME, November 15, 1910.

Berson, David. "Nav Problem: Schooner *Thomas W. Lawson.*" *Ocean Navigator,* Number 131. Portland, ME, July/August 2003.

Betlock, Lynn. *New England Ancestors* 4 (2003); 2:22-24, via internet: http://www.greatmigration.org/new_englands_great_migration.html.

Black, Colonel Frederick Fraser. *Searsport Sea Captains.* Searsport: 1960, page 83.

Boston Globe, Boston, September 9, 1902.

Boston Sunday Globe, Boston, June 24, 1973.

Bowley, R.L. *Isles of Scilly.* St. Mary's, Cornwall, England: Bowley Publications Ltd., 1999.

Bowley, R.L. *The Fortunate Islands: The Story of the Isles of Scilly.* St. Mary's, Cornwall, England: Bowley Publications Ltd., 1998, especially pages 110-136.

Brandon, Robin. *Isles of Scilly.* St. Ives, Cambridgeshire, England: Imray Laurie Norie & Wilson Ltd., 1999.

Bruzelius, Lars. "Sailing Ships: 'Thomas W. Lawson' (1902)," and "Schooners." *The Maritime History Vertical Archives,* via Internet: udac.se:8001/WWW/NauticalShips/Schooners/TWL(masts).html, September 14, 2002.

Buffalo Currier Express, Buffalo, August 31, 1961.

Caldarone, Richard. *Ancestors of Richard E. Dow.* Danvers, MA: Excerpts from family genealogy to the author via E-mail, 2004-2015.

Chapelle, Howard I. *The History of American Sailing Ships.* New York: W.W. Norton & Company, Inc., 1935.

Cooke, Anthony. "Taking Risks: The Great Ship Designers & Builders." *Seaport Magazine,* Winter/Spring 2006, pages 6-7.

Cornwell, E.L. (Editor). *The Illustrated History of Ships.* London: Octopus Books Limited, 1979, page 54 (*Lawson*) and 425-28 (*Torrey Canyon*).

Crabtree, Alfred B., and Martin, Hattie B. *Hancock 1828-1928.* Augusta, Me.: Kennebec Journal Company, 1928.

Crowe, Mike. "Droughers, Limers, and Packets." *Fishermen's Voice*, Volume 5 Number 3. Gouldsboro, ME: March 2000.

Crowinshield, Bowdoin B. *Fore and Afters.* Boston: Houghton, Mifflin & Co., 1940.

Cutter, William Richard (editor). *New England Families.* New York: Lewis Historical Publishing Company, 1914, Volume III, page 1137.

"Disaster at Scilly." *Western Weekly News.* Plymouth, England: December 21, 1907.

Daily Press, Newport News, Virginia, November 12, 1910, Volume 15, page 1.

Dow, Joseph, and Lucy Ellen Dow. *History of the Town of Hampton, New Hampshire, From Its Settlement in 1638 to the Autumn of 1892, Vol. II.* Salem, MA: Salem Press Printing and Publishing Co., 1893.

Dow, Henry. *Directory of American Biography.* New York: Charles Scribner's Sons, 1930, page 409.

Dow, Richard E. (Unpublished). Letter to Howard L. Jennings, July 1, 1954.

Dow, Robert Piercy. *The book of Dow: genealogical memoirs of the descendants of Henry Dow 1637, Thomas Dow 1639 and others of the name, immigrants to America during Colonial times, also the allied family of Nudd.* Claremont, N.H.: Robert P. Dow and Susan F. Dow (publishers), 1929.

Dyal, Donald H. "Death of a Schooner." Mystic, CT: *The Log of Mystic Seaport* Volume 35, Number 3, Fall 1983.

Dyer, Barbara F. *Village Soup.* Camden, ME, via Internet: Camden.villagesoup.com/opinions/GuestCols. efm?StoryID=2052.

Ellsworth American. Articles, advertisements, obituaries, etc., including September 27, 1905; August 11, 1983; 1936; October 11, 1952; October 23, 1955.

Fairburn, William Armstrong. *Merchant Sail,* Volumes I-VI. Center Lovell, Me.: Fairburn Marine Educational Foundation, Inc., 1897.

Falconer, John. *Sail & Steam, A Century of Seafaring Enterprise.* London: Viking, The Penguin Group, 1993.

Farnham, Monte. "The Wreck of the *Lawson*," *Skipper Magazine*, December 1967.

Foster, Richard. *Innovation.* New York: Summit Books, 1986, Chapter One.

Foster, Richard, and Kaplan, Sarah. *Creative Destruction.* New York: Doubleday, 2001.

Geni; MyHeritage Ltd. [www.geni.com]

Gillis, Richard (Unpublished). *A Graphic Account of the 'Loss of the* Thomas W. Lawson.' A monograph by Mr. Gillis, written in the late 1950's.

Gillis, Richard. *Western Morning News.* Plymouth, February 19,1958.

Goss, Elbridge Henry. *The History of Melrose, County of Middlesex, Massachusetts.* Melrose, Massachusetts: City of Melrose (publisher), 1902, pages 365 and 442.

Guide to Sailing Ship Rigs infosheet. Via Internet: museum.gov. ns.ca/mma/AtoZ/rigs.html

Hall, Thomas. *The T.W. Lawson: The Fate of the World's only Seven-Masted Schooner.* St. Johns, U.S.V.I.: Orchid Hill Publishing, 2003.

Havasy, Sena Spear, KnoxGen Web Co-ordinator. Isle au Haut: USGenWeb, On Line Genealogy Page, July 21, 2011. http://www. senahavasy.org/Isle_au_Haut.html.

Hazegray & Underway Shipbuilding Pages. Via Internet: Hazegray. org/shipbuilding/quincy.

Hicks, John, QC. *An Absolute Wreck.* United Kingdom: Scotforth Books, 2015.

Hicks, John H. (Unpublished). *The Wreck of the TW Lawson.* A monograph by Mr. Hicks of St. Agnes. St. Mary's: Isles of Scilly Museum.

Historical Society of the Town of Hancock. Various unpublished letters of Richard E. Dow, Gerard E. Graves, Ernestine Bushe Graves, Isadora A. Wooster, 1916-1957.

Hooper, William T. "My Years Before the Mast: Memoirs of Chesapeake Bay Waterman," Chapter I. Via Internet: freepages. genealogy.rootsweb.com/~fassitt/hooper/hooper_01.html.

Hornsby, Thomas. "The Last Voyage of The Thomas W. Lawson." *Nautical Research Journal,* Volume V, Number 4. Brighton, MA: Nautical Research Guild, Inc., April 1953.

Hosmer, George L. *Historical Sketch of the Town of Deer Isle, Maine.* Sunset, ME: Deer Isle-Stonington Historical Society, 1983.

Immigrant Ships Transcribers Guild, Volume 5. National Archives and Records Administration, Film M277, Reel 115, List 158.

Jennings, Howard L. (Unpublished). Letters to Richard E. Dow, December 11, 1953; April 2, 1954; May 11, 1954; June 4, 1954; June 28, 1954.

Klosterman, Chuck. *Abandon Ship.* The New York Sunday Times Magazine, May 25, 2014, page 14.

Larn, Richard (Editor). *Ships, Shipwrecks & Maritime Incidents Around the Isles of Scilly.* St. Mary's: Isles of Scilly Museum Publication No. 3 (revised edition), 1999.

Little, George Thomas (editor). *Genealogical and Family History.* New York: Lewis Historical Publishing Company, 1909, "Dow" entries.

Maine History on Line, Maine Memory Network; Maine Historical Society, 2000-2015 [http://www.mainememory.net]

Massachusetts On the Sea 1630-1930. Boston: The Commonwealth of Massachusetts, 1930.

"Mauritania I, 1907-1935." *Cunard Heritage*. Via Internet: /.../indexcfm?method=legacyship&sLang=us&content=legacy&shipline=home&shipid=10, August 30, 2001.

Men Ships and the Sea. Chicago: National Geographic Society, 1962.

Merrill, Peter. *State of Mind* (Manuscript). Portland, ME: 2004.

Miller, Florence Carleton. Sail plan, Rockport, ME, 1967.

Minutes of the Meeting of the Trustees (Unpublished). Boston Marine Society. Boston, December 8, 1891.

Moon, T.C. "Breakers Ahead." *The Ellsworth American.* Ellsworth, Me.: August 4, 1926.

National Weather Service Chicago. *The Beaufort Wind Scale.* Via Internet: Crh.noaa.gov/lot/webpage/beaufort.

Nielsen, Eric. "Niels Anton Nielsen," via Internet: milhist.dk/ soldiers/port/Nielsen.htm, January 29, 2003.

Obituary of Captain George W. Dow. *Melrose Free Press.* Melrose, MA: March 21, 1919.

Parry, John H. *Romance of the Sea.* Washington, D.C.: National Geographic Society, 1981.

Quinn, B.F. Excerpts from family genealogy via Internet: home.attbi.com/~bfquinn83/d69.htm, and home.comcast. net/~bfquinn83/personas/lawson_story.htm.

Quinn, B.F. Excerpts from narrative regarding the *Thomas W. Lawson* and Captain George w. Dow, and including excerpts from *American Neptune,* and *The Sicillonian* (Trevellick Moyle, Autumn, 1960), via Interned: http://home.comcast. net/~bfquinn83/personal/gwd_narrative.htm, and /Lawson_ narrative.htm.

Quinn, David M. *Leviathan's Master.* Bloomington, IN: iUniverse, 2009.

Record of American and Foreign Shipping. New York: American Bureau of Shipping, 1867-1920.

Registry of Graduates, Massachusetts Institute of Technology. Boston: Geo. H. Ellis Co., 1904.

"Report on Ship Registers—Auburndale." Bath, ME: Penobscott Marine Museum, June 4, 1941.

Ronnberg, Erik A.R. Jr. "Stranger in Truth than in Fiction: The American Seven-Masted Schooners." *Nautical Research Journal*, vol. 38, No. 1, March 1993, pp. 5-41.

Roorda, Curtis (Transcriber). "Immigrant Ships Transcribers Guild—Bark Auburndale." National Archives and Records Administration, Film M277, Reel 115, List 158. Via Internet: Istg. rootsweb.com/v5/1800v5/auburndale18910603.html, September 21, 2002.

Rowe, William Hutchinson. *The Maritime History of Maine.* Gardiner, Me.: The Harpswell Press, 1948.

Sandstrom, Fredrik. "Schooners." *Sailing Ships, 2000.* Via Internet: Infa.abo.fi/~fredrik/sships/schooners.html.

"Schooner Lawson Wrecked; 15 Drown." *New York Times.* New York: December 15, 2007.

Smith, Sam. "Ghosts." *Multitudes: The Unauthorized Memoirs of Sam Smith.* Via Internet: prorev.com/mmghosts.htm, February 8, 2003.

Snow, Edward Rowe. *Great Sea Rescues,* Chapter 17. New York: Dodd, Mead & Company, 1958.

Tam, Kevin R. "Ships of State: RMS Mauretania." Via Internet: Uncommonjourneys.com/pages/mauretania.hem, 1997.

"The Beaufort Wind Scale." Chicago: National Weather Service, via Internet: crh.noaa.gov/lot/webpage/beaufort.

"The Glamorous Six Masters." Via Internet: afn.org.~stan/ships.html, September 16, 2002.

"The R.N.L.I. on Scilly," via Internet: members.aol.com/simcross/maritime/rboats.html.

The Sailor's Magazine and Seamen's Friend, Volume 71. New York: American Seamen's Friend Society, 1899, page 69.

"The Schooner 'Thomas W. Lawson.'" Notes From the Seamen's Bank for Savings (Fine Arts Collection), 1975.

The Shoe and Leather Reporter, Volume 57. Boston: May 17, 1894, page 1122.

The Technology Review. Cambridge, MA: The Alumni Association of the Massachusetts Institute of Technology, 1917, Volume XIX, page 315.

"Thomas W. Lawson." *Dictionary of American Biography.* Via Internet: millicentlibrary.org/Lawson-b.htmm 1933.

Toppan, Andrew. *The Portland Gale.* Haze Gray & Underway Photo Feature, 1998.

Wasson, Samuel, "Survey of Hancock County, Maine" (1878). Maine History Documents. Paper 37.

Wigglesworth, Angela. *People of Scilly.* Dover, NH: Alan Sutton Publishing, Inc., 1995.

Wilson, Neil. *Great Sea Disasters*. Bristol, Great Britain: Siena/ Parragon, 1998, p. 27.

ILLUSTRATION SOURCES

1. Title page (GWD portrait). Dow family collection.

2. Dedication page (GWD on deck). Dow family collection.

3. Page X (Three boys in Scilly). Turner family collection.

4. Page XIV (*Lawson*). Revue Générale de la Marine Marchande 1901, accessed at https://escales.files.wordpress.com/2015/01/thomas-w-lawson-revue-gc3a9n-c3a9rale-de-la-marine-marchande-1901.jpg.

5. Page 3 (*Mayflower II*). Plimoth Plantation, accessed at http://www.connect-icutmag.com/Blog/History/December-2014/The-Mayflower-IIs-Unlikely-Jour-ney-to-Mystic-Seaport/MayflowerIIcourtseyplimothplantation.jpg.

6. Page 5 (Yarmouth to Watertown map). Curt Carpenter.

7. Page 6 (English village). Plimoth Plantation, accessed at http://media.photo-bucket.com/user/FreedomJourneyOutpost/media/13%20Colony%20Journey%20Plymouth/IMG_1410_zpse05e79d0.jpg.html?filters[term]=plymouth%20colo-ny%20houses&filters[primary]=images.

8. Page 10 (New Hampshire coast towns map). Curt Carpenter.

9. Page 13 (New Hampshire to Deer Isle map). Curt Carpenter.

10. Page 14 (Deer Isle bridge). Turner family collection.

11. Page 15 (New Meadows River). Turner family collection.

12. Page 16 (Dow Rd. sign). Turner family collection.

13. Page 17 (Deer Isle to Hancock map). Curt Carpenter.

14. Page 19 (Isle au Haute). Turner family collection.

15. Page 20 (Dow Point Road sign). Turner family collection.

16. Page 20 (Maine seal). Public domain.

17. Page 21 (Somes Sound). Turner family collection.

18. Page 23 (Dows Way sign). Turner family collection.

19. Page 24 (Hancock sign). Turner family collection.

20. Page 27 (Ten generation summary). Turner family analysis.

21. Page 29 (Young GWD). Calderone family collection.

22. Page 34 (Hancock and Ellsworth map). Curt Carpenter.

23. Page 35 (bible). Turner family collection.

24. Page 37 (Ellsworth lot). S. F. Colby & Co., publishers, Ellsworth Village Plan No. 1, 1881.

25. Page 37 (Ellsworth sign). Turner family collection.

26. Page 38 (Ellsworth corner). Turner family collection.

27. Page 46 (Bar Harbor train). New England Steam Corporation, accessed at http://www.acadiavisitor.com/wp-content/uploads/sites/18/2015/05/crt-en-gine-470.jpg.

28. Page 49 (Melrose house). Street view by maps.google.com, copyright 2015.

29. Page 51 (*Butler*). Photo from www.wrecksite.eu/img/wrecks/gale08.

30. Page 53 (*Auburndale*). Turner family collection.

31. Page 55 (top hat). Turner family collection.

32. Page 56 (planter's chair). Turner family collection.

33. Page 58 (BMS certificate). Turner family collection.

34. Page 60 (Richard portraits). Turner family collection.

35. Page 62 (GWD, Prentiss with old car). Calderone family collection.

36. Page 67 (Bath sign). Turner family collection.

37. Page 68 (five schooners). Courtesy, The Mariners' Museum, Newport News, Virginia.

38. Page 70 (Percy & Small sign). Turner family collection.

39. Page 71 (*Lawson*). Original source uncertain; Calderone family collection; also appears in Quinn, David M. *Leviathan's Master*. Bloomington, IN: iUniverse, 2009, page 26.

40. Page 72 (stateroom). Peabody & Essex Museum.

41. Page 75 (Thomas *Lawson*). Photo in Harris & Ewing Collection (Library of Congress), dated 1918.

42. Page 76 (*Lawson*). Page 76 (*Lawson*). Photographer unknown, possibly

N.L. Stebbins or shipyard's photographer, accessed at www.hazegray.org/ship-building/quincy/images/lawson.jpg."

43. Page 87 (Philadelphia to Scilly map). Curt Carpenter.

44. Page 94 (Dogs of Scilly). Postcard, The "Neptune" Series by C. King, Scilly Isles, copyright photograph, Turner family collection.

45. Page 95 (St. Agnes Lighthouse). Alamy photo accessed at http://www.dailymail.co.uk/news/article-2454631/Baby-born-remote-island-St-Agnes-Scillies-1927.html.

46. Page 96 (Bishop Rock Lighthouse). http://news.bbc.co.uk/local/cornwall/hi/people_and_places/history/newsid_8470000/8470873.stm.

47. Page 104 (Jack Hicks). Harris, Keith. "Azook: The Story of the Pilot Gigs of Cornwall and the Isles of Scilly 1666–1994", 1994, Dyllansow Truran publishers (out of print). Accessed at http://www.pilotmag.co.uk/2008/01/08/pilot-gigs-of-cornwall-and-the-scilly-isles/.

48. Page 106 (capsized hull). Photo copyright F.E. Gibson, Scilly Isles, courtesy Sotheby's, accessed at http://www.huffingtonpost.com/2013/10/26/shipwreckphotos_n_4159543.

49. Page 109 (Scilly Isles map). Curt Carpenter.

50. Page 111 (*Slippen*). Original photo source unknown. Accessed at http://talesofriverside.blogspot.com/2007/08/seven-masted-schooner-thomas-lawson.html.

51. Page 114 (Scilly Isles map). Curt Carpenter.

52. Page 117 (life preserver). Photo in Turner family collection; taken at Valhalla Museum, Tresco Abbey Gardens, Isles of Scilly.

53. Page 119 (pocket watch). Photo on ebay, July 28, 2016 sale, accessed at http://www.cafr.ebay.ca/itm/Complete-POCKET-WATCH-THOMAS-W-LAWSON-American-shipwreck-1907-/351789103070?hash=item51e843b7de:g:3QkAAOSwdzVXkIOz.

54. Page 121 (Eternal Father). "Eternal Father—The 'Navy Hymn.'" Navy FAQ, accessed at chinfo.navy.mil/navpalib/questions/eternal.html, September 14, 2002; and "Eternal Father, Strong to Save." Accessed at cyberhymnal.org/htm/e/t/eternal.htm, September 14, 2002.

55. Page 125 (clay pipe). Turner family collection.

56. Page 126 (Hicks receipt). Calderone family collection.

57. Page 136 (*Torrey Canyon*). Photographer unidentified, accessed at http://

www.divernet.com/img/66/800/600/0/85679/187762.jpg.

58. Page 136 (Djibouti stamp). Turner family collection.

59. Page 136 (Congo coin). Photo on ebay, accessed at http://www.ebay. com/itm/1-000-SILVER-FRANCS-1-000-FRANCOS-PLATA-CONGO-2001-THOMAS-W-LAWSON-PROOF-/281292523170.

60. Page 137 (*Mauretania*). Image of vintage postcard, source unknown, accessed at https://www.flickr.com/photos/adambangor/5334219126.

61. Page 141 (*Philadelphia*). Print of painting by Antonio Nicolo Gasparo Jacobsen "The American Liner Philadelphia 1902".

62. Page 142 (*Calumet*). Photo courtesy of Maine Maritime Museum, Bath, Maine.

63. Page 143 (*Inez N. Carver*). Photo courtesy of Maine Maritime Museum, Bath, Maine.

64. Page 145 (GWD, Jennie portraits). Turner family collection.

65. Page 146 (Deputy Sheriff certificate). Turner family collection.

66. Page 149 (Girard's cabin). Turner family collection.

67. Page 150 (Girard with shotgun). *Bangor Daily News*, October 11, 1952.

68. Page 151 (Taunton River tide). Turner family collection.

69. Page 152 (Gravestone). Turner family collection.

www.ingramcontent.com/pod-product-compliance
Lightning Source LLC
Chambersburg PA
CBHW041829090426
42811CB00038B/2365/J